SIXTEEN SERMONS

Sixteen prayers, from the Old and New Testament

Louis Neely

Prayer Sixteen Sermons

Copyright © 2015 by Louis Neely

All rights reserved. No part of this publication may be reproduced, distributed or transmitted in any form or by any means, without prior written permission.

Sangre Publishing
9933 Business Park Drive
Sacramento, CA 95827
warehousechristianministries.org

ISBN: 978-0-9968575-0-5

TABLE OF CONTENTS

CONVERSATION WITH GOD 1
    Adam and Eve 1
JACOB'S PRAYER 11
    Wrestling with God 11
THE PITIFUL PRAYER 21
    Moses 21
THE GOD OF OPPORTUNITY 33
    Jabez, the Poor Son 33
KING ASA'S PRAYER 41
    Righteous Reform 41
DANIEL'S PRAYER FOR UNDERSTANDING 51
    Bible Prophecy 51
THE PRAYER OF HEALING 61
    Demons and Disciples 61
PRAYER FOR OUR DAILY NEEDS 69
    Bread, Temptation, Forgiveness 69
PERSISTENT PRAYER 79
    Knock and Ask 79
PRAY OR LOSE HEART 89
    When There's No Place to Turn 89

THE UPPER ROOM DISCOURSE...................99
   Greater Works Than These...........................99
KEPT IN CHRIST...107
   Able to Keep You From Falling....................107
PURPOSE OF PRAYER................................117
   Mission of the Church.............................117
PRAYER WILL KEEP THE DOOR OPEN 127
   Prayer in Persecution.............................127
THREE PHASES OF PRAYER 137
   Supplication, Intercession, Thanksgiving. 137
PRAY NOT TO BE RICH 149
   Materialism or Spirituality 149

To my wife and best friend, Mary. Without her faith and help this book would not be possible, nor would my life and ministry be as fruitful.

CONVERSATION WITH GOD
Adam and Eve
Genesis 3:8-13

I have been blessed over the last few weeks, spending a good deal of time studying about prayer in both the Old and the New Testament. It is a life changing experience to go through the Word and begin to put prayer into practice. And to see the dynamics, the power, the miraculous happenings that take place when the church makes prayer its number one priority.

Lord, we thank you for who you are. And for the miraculous and wonderful access you've given us into your presence. For the spirit of forgiveness, Lord, I ask your forgiveness for my negligence in prayer. For letting my mind be wrapped up in the cares of this life, the deceitfulness of riches, and the lust of things, until the Word becomes stifled. Lord, I want to reach out to you and enter into a deeper relationship with you through prayers. So I pray that you will guide me, that you will guide all of us, that we might experience the joy of being in fellowship with you. We ask this in Jesus' name, Amen.

This morning I want to start teaching from the Book of Genesis, Chapter 3. When we read the first prayer recorded in the Bible, at first it may not seem like a prayer at all. But it is. This raises the question; what constitutes prayer? Prayer is simply a conversation between two people; between you and God. It is a private conversation, even when you are in the midst of people. But even in corporate prayer, our prayer is individual, reaching up and speaking to and receiving communication from God.

The more you pray the more you will learn to hear God's voice, you will begin to recognize His promptings, and His guidance, and His leadership. So there are only two people in true prayer; the person who is praying, and the God whom they are addressing. There can be others around, but it's only you and God.

There are many forms of prayer, and we're going to be getting into that later on future Sundays. For this morning, we just need to accept that prayer is a simple conversation, a dialogue between God and man. Prayer is integral to our being. I am convinced that at times of crisis even atheists pray. I am always amazed when there is a public figure who suffers great illness, or tragedy, or death, you hear people say "We will remember you in our prayers." Whether they do or not I don't know, but you hear it all the time.

Jesus spoke famous words on prayer in the Sermon on the Mount. This is in the sixth chapter of Matthew, in the sixth verse. He said, "When you pray," and in the King James it said, "Go into your closet and shut the door." In other translations it will say "Go into your room." When it talks about going into your closet it is not literally to go into the closet; closets are normally very crowded and uncomfortable. And so you begin to think about that; when you pray go in your closet and shut the door. I can remember early in my ministry I took that literally. I would cram into a closet in the motel room if they had one, and spend time in prayer.

But you realize after a while that's not what God is talking about. He is talking about shutting the door to shut everyone and everything else out. To focus your mind, and your attention, upon the Father, upon the Son as the Holy Spirit. Because this helps us to pray. Don't let anything interfere in your time of prayer. It is vital as Christians that we do this. I can tell you right now that I do not spend as much time in prayer as I would like. My prayer life is not as strong as it should be, and you may well agree with that in your own life.

Shut everything else out. Don't think about other things, don't think about people, focus your attention on God. I was watching the candidates shake hands the other day as they were trying to get votes, and I noticed that they would try their best to look right in that person's eye. But it wouldn't be long before most of them were looking somewhere else, and thinking "Okay, I shook this hand, how many more are here? How many votes do I have here?" and so forth.

And I am not putting them down; what a tough thing to do, to run for public office in this country. My goodness, you know by the time you get through with all the scrutiny and everything, you got to end up feeling like a hair on a biscuit; you really do. It's just one of the horrible things that they go through, and you pray for them, because we need good public servants. But when we talk to God, just focus our attention on Him.

Adam and Eve had been put in this perfect place. They had work to do that was fulfilling, they had fellowship with God, who would come down in the form of a man walking with them in the cool of the evening. I know the Bible doesn't literally say that, but I believe that's what it means, because the scripture says, "They would hear his footsteps." Perhaps this was just a prelude or a hint of the incarnation that was to come; God would appear in the form of a man, and someday when Christ came He would appear as a man. For Adam and Eve it was a joyous time of fellowship with God. During this early time God would speak to them, but prayer had not originated because it was only God speaking; it was not a dialogue, a conversation between God and Adam and Eve.

Then they sinned. For the first time, sin entered into paradise. The Bible said that God told them they can have anything, and do anything, in this beautiful garden, with its perfect temperature, everything perfect... except one thing; they must not eat of the fruit of the tree of knowledge, of good and evil. For when they do that, they are attempting to become like God. And from that day to this, man has struggled with trying to become his own God. Trying to have the position that only God Himself deserves, that only God Himself can fill.

So now they had sinned, and God speaks to them. The scriptures says, "But when you pray, shut your closet door and communicate with me." Adam and Eve had looked forward every day to that time in the cool of the evening when God would come and literally walk with them, and talk with them, and have this marvelous relationship with them; but now because of sin, they begin to hide. When we've done something wrong we don't want to face it, that's our nature. If you've ever been on a long diet, you know when you are losing weight you can't wait to hit the scales; but when you feel like you might be gaining, you stop weighing. You ever noticed that? And you stop talking about how much you weigh. When you are going down you say, "Oh boy, that looks good today". And when you start going the other way you say. "Whoa, whoa, I need to start another diet tomorrow", and another five years passes and you start all over again. So it was with Adam and Eve; they had sinned, and they no longer wanted to face God.

The scripture said in Chapter 3, verses 8 and 9, "And they heard the sound of the Lord, God walking in the garden in the cool of the day, and Adam and Eve hid themselves from the presence of God among the trees of the garden. And then the Lord asked Adam a question. He said, "Adam, where are you?" This was the beginning of prayer. God initiated the conversation. God always initiates prayer, even though you might think you are, it is God who stirs us to pray. Then it's up to us to see whether we pray or we don't pray.

Being with God had been a part of their life, walking in the cool of the evening from the time they were created, and now all of a sudden they hid from God. The sound of the footsteps reminded Adam and Eve that this was the time of day that God came to have fellowship with them, but all of a sudden they didn't want to face God. So they hid, because they knew they had done the one thing that God told them not to do. You ever noticed that when you grow cold in your spirit one of the first things you do is drop out of church? Second thing you begin to do is withdraw socially from your Christian friends. You stay out of the Word of God, you stop praying. It's a progression. And what is happening is, that we are separating ourselves from the presence of God, because intuitively, in our spirit, we are ashamed of what we are doing. Sin can be defined as anything that separates us from the presence of Holy

God. If there is anything in our lives that makes us reluctant to be in the presence of God, or open to the Word, or to spend time in prayer, it is sin. That's what Satan wants to do; he wants to separate us and make us vulnerable. Adam and Eve didn't want to face God, but they needed a conversation with God, so God initiated that conversation.

Sometimes we get the wrong idea about God. When Abraham was praying that God would spare the city of Sodom and Gomorrah, that the angel of the Lord would withhold judgment that was coming, Abraham started off saying "God I know you, you would never bring judgment upon the righteous with the unrighteous. If there are even fifty righteous men, would you spare Sodom and Gomorrah?" God said "Yes, I would." Abraham then tried forty-five, forty, and down, until finally it got to ten. Somebody said that if Abraham had continued to pray, had he kept the number lower and lower, Sodom and Gomorrah would have been saved. But I don't believe that; I believe God had reached a point in His life, for Sodom and Gomorrah's sin was such that God knew they were beyond repentance. They had crossed that final line where God said, "Alright, grace and mercy have lifted, and now judgment will come."

I know many people think it was because of the homosexual sin, but that wasn't it at all, because you look at the scripture in Matthew 11:24 and it says, "Woe to you Bethsaida. I say to you, it shall be more tolerable for the land of Sodom on the day of judgment, than for you." In other words, you're in greater sin. Why? Because they had had miracles and marvelous things happen in Bethsaida, as the ministry of Christ when He walked the earth. And God was saying, "You've had so many opportunities, had the same miracles taken place in Sodom and Gomorrah they would have repented in sackcloth and ashes. But instead you have rebelled against me and so your judgment will be greater."

I am going to tell you what I know. I know in my spirit, I know in my heart that when it comes to America, if we turn up in the judgment seat of God, the great white throne judgment, our judgment will be harsher than others; because we have had more opportunities to know God, and to receive God, and open our lives to God, than any other nation on earth. That's how God looks at it.

But God knew Sodom had reached that point when the only thing that would work, the only thing that would be a warning to others, was that judgment would come. God had determined that city was beyond redemption. Man is never more compassionate than God. It's not that we come in and say, "God spare this, spare that, spare something else." No. If we pray and we have love and compassion, that all comes from God, it's not from us.

The scripture tells us in 1 John Chapter 4 and verse 7, "Beloved, let us love one another, for love is of God, and everyone who loves is born of God, and knows God." If you love people deeply - not just your family, or those who can benefit you, but if you love the human race deeply, that doesn't come from you or I, it doesn't come from our human flesh, it comes from God!

God is the one who gives us love, God is the one who makes us care about the needs of others. God's love in us. He helps us when we want to pray, and to seek out and to reach out to Him in prayer. Romans 8:26 says, "Likewise, the Spirit also helps in our weakness, for we do not know what we should pray for as we ought, but the Spirit himself makes intercessions for us with groanings that cannot be uttered."

Sometimes the heavy burden rests upon our hearts, until we can't say anything. We just cry in our spirit and we groan in our spirit, "Lord, answer a prayer, this need is great, this challenge is imminent, Lord without your intervention there is no hope." And I pray that way many times in my life. I have seen God move, but it is the Holy Spirit that helps us to pray.

When God asks Adam the question "Where are you?" it wasn't because He needed information. He knew where Adam was. He knew where Adam was, but he still asked; "Adam where are you?" Why? He was asking a powerful question. Where are you and I in our walk with God? Where are we now in our journey into eternity? What is our relationship with God? Are we stronger with God now than we were at any point in our life in the past?

There's one thing about being a Christian, you're either growing or you are dying. You are getting stronger, or weaker; spiritual weakness coming into our lives.

In Genesis 3:10, the excuses begin. Adam said "I heard your voice in the garden and I was afraid because I was naked and I hid myself." Well, Adam and Eve had been naked since they were created. And God asked him the question, "Who told you, you were naked?" How did you know the difference between being clothed and naked?" You see, there was an outside force that they were listening to, and God was leading them in prayer, to prompt them into an acknowledgement. Who told you that you were naked? And then in the 13th verse He asked a question, "What is that you have done?" What have *you* done? Not "What has somebody else done."

In Job Chapter 38 verse 3, God always knows the answer in advance. Job had gone through so much suffering, and so many trials, that all of a sudden he just said, "If I could just get a hold of God I would ask Him some questions and I would call God into account." Have you ever been in that place in your life? "When I get to heaven I am going to ask God this or that or something else."

God said now wait a minute, Job 38:3; He said, effectively, now prepare yourself like a man and get on your feet. I will question you and you will answer me. That's what God said to Job. You want to ask me questions? Well I am going to start, because I am the one that's talking to you. God has basically said, bring it on Job. Bring it on. And He begins to ask a series of scientific questions that Job couldn't answer. He asked, "Where were you when I laid out the foundations of the earth?" And you should read that 38th chapter of Job this afternoon if you're having questions that you want God to answer, go through the 38th chapter. What happened to Job when it came his turn to answer? The Bible said he fell on his face in sackcloth and ashes and said, "Oh God, I am a wretched sinner, please forgive me and deliver me from the bondage of my sin."

Adam begins to answer God. God said, "Adam, where are you?" Adam said "I heard your voice in the garden and I was afraid because I was naked and so I hid myself." He asked a question, "Where are you?" And I am asking you the question, "Where are you in your relationship with God?" Are you hiding from God? Getting wrapped up in things, trying to ignore God, trying to act as though you are an immortal that you will live forever, that you will never die. That you will never face eternity in heaven or hell? Are you hiding from God? Am I hiding from God?

Where are you in your life in relationship to God? Prayer is where you will find the answer. And prayer is where you will find mercy. And grace, and deliverance.

Now Adam and Eve had shame. "I am naked." Somebody told me I was naked and I looked around and sure enough, I was. I am naked. Excuses, excuses. So what did Adam say to God? The same thing we've been saying for years; the woman whom you gave to be with me, she gave me of the tree. It was the woman who did it.

And God said to the woman, "What is this you have done?" And the woman said, "The serpent deceived me." So Adam had a woman to blame, and Eve had a snake. But here is the problem; when he said "It's the woman you gave me" he made this three-word statement; "And I ate." And Eve also said, "And I ate." In those three words they acknowledged, whether they knew it or not, that they were responsible for sin in their life. You can blame the hypocrite preachers - and you are looking at one right here… for a hypocrite is one who does not always live up to everything they profess. Which is all of us. You can blame your mother, or dad. Or your harsh treatment as a child, too many spankings of a cruel father or cruel mother. And those are horrible burdens to bear. But God can heal you of that. The fact is, it's up to you whether you eat or not. Whether you partake of a rebellion against God.

"And I ate." But with confession came forgiveness, and God prepared clothing for them. And God said, you are going to go through these trials, and you going to go through these terrible tests, because of sin. But He also said, I am also going to walk with you, and you can be with me. And He cursed the one who was a part of the problem, the serpent. He placed a curse on him. God was saying, "Yes, you're going through trials but I still love you."

And I still want to have fellowship with you, and I am still going to be with you, and I am still going to walk with you, and I am going to prepare for you the things that you need. And I will never leave you nor forsake you, in spite of your sin.

When you ask forgiveness, you will receive forgiveness. I don't care what you've done or what you fail to do; whether it's the sins of omission or commission, God will forgive and God will deliver you. But the question I want you to ask yourself this morning has been burning in my heart for weeks now; where are you with God? I love these people in this church. I love people period. Not because of the thing in my nature, but because God fills my heart with His love for people. His patience, His tolerance.

And I wonder, and I am asking you as the pastor that cares; how often do you pray? How often do you enter dialogue with God? How often do you communicate with God? Is God an afterthought? You just come to church once in a while, or maybe regularly, but don't have that daily personal intimate fellowship with Jesus. God wants you, and longs for you, and is lonely for you. Shut the door, turn off your television, lay down the magazines. There are a thousand voices in our culture, "Come vacation here because you deserve it; come buy this to eat because you deserve it; buy this car and you will find happiness; take this product and it will transform your life." And they are lies.

I had a friend call me up just a few weeks ago, and I love him, I love him like a brother, and he said, "I have money by the millions". He said, "I pay more taxes than I thought I would ever make in money," and he said, "Money is nothing. Money means nothing." And I heard the cry, and the emptiness in his life and in his soul, as he called late in the night and said, "I need help". He didn't say that out loud, but I heard it. "I need help, I need God. I have everything materially and more than I ever dreamed of or wanted but I am empty." Only God can fill the human spirit and soul, and give us lasting peace.

Where are you? If you have been shutting God out of your life, it is time for confession, and you will receive forgiveness. Lord, there is no one else, there is nothing else but me that keeps me away from time in prayer. Forgive me for every decision that I make without consulting you, forgive me for letting other things fill my mind so completely that it shuts out your voice. Lord, you have given everything for me, and for us, and we give so little back. We confess our spiritual poverty. Oh Lord, take the clutter out of our lives and make us rich in God. May the fellowship be restored. And then when you are asked the question, "Where are you?" You will say, "Lord, I am right here beside you. What would you have me do? Where would you have me be? For I and everything you have entrusted me with belongs to you. For every good and perfect gift comes from you."

Lord, teach us to pray.

JACOB'S PRAYER
Wrestling with God
Genesis 32:6-29

This morning the title of the message is Jacob's Prayer. I, unfortunately relate to Jacob. A lot of the problems that he had, I have. I just want to end up like he did. God works with us through our personalities, and through all the foibles of our life. And ultimately as we walk with Him, if we are faithful and just keep our hearts and lives in tune with Him, He will get us where He wants us to be; and that's in His presence for eternity. That's God ultimate goal for all of us.

We talked last week about the fact that man does not, if you really study the Bible, he does not initiate prayer. God initiates prayer. If you have a desire to pray or need to pray, God is the one who created that desire in you, who stirred you. Prayer is a conversation between man and God. You talk to God, you listen, and you seek His guidance, His wisdom. And we're hoping that as we go through these series we will learn how to pray in a Biblical fashion, and that our prayers will be more fruitful.

There are some people who wonder whether God hears those who are non-believers, or of different religions. I believe the answer is yes. There is a scripture in Psalm 65:2 that says, "Oh thou that hearest prayer unto thee shall all flesh come." Oh thou that hearest prayer. God does hear prayers. He heard your prayer when you were in rebellion against God, you had no personal relationship with Jesus; He heard your prayer. It may have been a sigh that says, "What does life mean? What is the meaning of my life? What is the purpose of my life?" That could be a prayer. God will lead you if you will listen, until you have a revelation of who

God is and how much He loves you, what He desires to do for our good in our lives.

In the New Testament, Cornelius was a pagan Roman, but he was influenced by the Jewish communion. He would attend some of the synagogues, and he learned about God, and he began to pray to Him. He wasn't a Christian at that time, he was a pagan. But in the Book of Acts the Bible said, "And when he observed Him he saw this angel, he was afraid and he said 'What is it Lord?' So He said to him 'Your prayers and your alms had come up for a memorial before God.'" God initiated the desire and the longing for prayer in that man's heart, and ultimately led him to faith. So God hears prayers.

A pastor was talking to an old sea captain, hearing about some of the terrible storms that he had experienced in his years as a captain. He talked about one particular storm that was so violent and wild, that even after all his years at sea he didn't think they were going to make it. And the pastor asked him "What did you learn in that?" He said, "Well, God heard from many strangers that night." I believe there is a time that even an atheist prays. There was an atheist rejoicing over the fact that we're no longer able to have prayers in the school, and he said, "One of the happiest days of my life." He said, "Thank God."

So there is a time in our life when we will pray, I truly believe that. This morning we pick up the story of Jacob in Genesis Chapter 32 and verse 6. Jacob had an interesting life. He was constantly maneuvering and manipulating people and circumstances for his own advantage, and he was good at it. He knew that the birthright came with a blessing from God, but he was a twin and he was the second, so that birthright actually belonged to his older brother Esau. But Esau didn't understand the benefits and how precious that birthright was, so Jacob deceived his brother. Jacob probably would have been the kind of guy in his early days that would have been on the Food Channel, he loved to cook. Esau was a hunter, and the scripture said, that for whatever purpose, it mentioned that he was a hairy man. He was a man of the field. He loved to hunt, and when he came in he was so hungry he could hardly wait for a bite. Jacob had a big pot of lentils, it smelled so good. And Esau said to Jacob "Let me have some," and Jacob said "Well, if you would sell or trade me for your birthright." Esau didn't have any sense of spiritual values whatsoever, he was a fleshly man, a carnal man. He said, "Oh sure I will sell it." So Jacob deceived his brother, to have the blessing that came with being the first born. He had to deceive his father too, who is now blind and old and aging. But Isaac still had a good sense of smell. So Jacob put some goatskin on his hands and arms. When his father would bless him he felt the hairy arms, he said, "Oh that's hairy Esau," and he blessed Jacob. Then Jacob had to flee for his life, because when Esau realized how he had been deceived and manipulated he was going to kill his brother. So Jacob took off.

Now Jacob had been gone at this time for about twenty years, working for his father-in-law, Laban. He now had two wives and eleven children. He also had become wealthy through outsmarting his father-in-law, Laban. He owned vast herds of cattle, and donkeys, and camels, and goats, and sheep. He had a vast army of servants to serve him, and now God had spoken to him and told him to go back. God said "If you go back to your land, I will bless you." And so Jacob was going back, but the tragedy is, in the twenty years when he had married and had his family, he had been away from God. His family was deeply involved in idolatry. They had to have a spiritual meeting, and that's the tragic thing. When we drift from God and we go out on our own, it doesn't just affect us, it affects our children and future generations.

There are some times we are totally faithful to God; as faithful as we know how to be. And still our children drift. But there is a promise; the Bible said, when they are old, at some point in their life they are going to come back. And I believe that. I have seen it over and over again through the years of pastoring here. People that went away, came back. So Jacob was headed back. Now some messengers came to Jacob. He was getting close, and he was afraid of his brother Esau. He thought he was going to surely be killed. And they came back and they said to Jacob, "We came to your brother Esau, and he also is coming to meet you with four hundred armed men." And that's not good news.

Though God had promised Jacob, Jacob truly did not really believe God. Yet now he makes this beautiful prayer. Jacob was wealthy, he had these great herds, he had his family, he had all of his servants, he had gone out with nothing but a staff to walk on; and now he is coming back a wealthy man. But Jacob thinks like a business man. He said "Well, I don't want to experience a total loss," so he divided his company in half. He sent one half one way, and one half the other, thinking that if Esau came and slaughtered one half he would still have half left. Not believing God, not trusting God.

Now he had cheated Esau, he'd deceived his father, he'd constantly manipulated people for his own gain, and now he was about to face his brother Esau, and he didn't think he would survive unless he did something. So Jacob the manipulator, the sleek business man, the guy that had outsmarted everybody and was admired for it, sounds like an American, Jacob saw the same thing that Elisha's servants saw when death threatened him. He wasn't alone; he wasn't outnumbered by fighting men, there was a whole host of angelic beings around him. Remember when the king was going to kill Elisha, and he sent the troops, and his servant was just absolutely freaking out? "We're gonna die." But Elisha said to Him, "Lord open his eyes" and he looked around and the hills were filled with chariots of fire and angelic beings, and the servant recognized "There are more for us than there are against us."

And that's exactly what's going on in your life, Christian of God; but open your eyes, and you would see that whatever your problems, whatever your challenges are, there are more for you than there are against you. And the ones for you can't be beat. But in spite of God's promise and provision, Jacob was afraid. When Jacob began to pray, he addressed God properly though. He did it the right way. Jacob said, Genesis 32:9, "Oh God of my father Abraham, and the God of my father Isaac, and the Lord who said to me, 'If you returned your company to your family I will deal well with you...'" So now he starts off by addressing God.

When you start to pray the first thing you do is address God. Jesus told us in the Book of Matthew; when you pray, start this way, "Our Father who art in heaven, hallowed be thy name," that's how we start our prayer. We know who we are talking to, we begin addressing God by giving Him honor, by acknowledging His power, His greatness and His mercy, and His ability to do anything. In Jacob's earlier prayer, found in Genesis 28: verses 20 to 22, he made a vow saying "If God will be with me and keep me in this way that I am going, and give me bread to eat and clothing to put on, so that I come back to my father's house in peace, then the Lord shall be my God and this stone which I set as a pillar shall be God's house. And that all that you give me I will surely give you a tenth, I will tithe." At that time Jacob was on his way away from home fleeing for his life, and all he had in his hand was a stick. God had blessed him, and now he had thousands of animals, a number of servants and eleven children and two wives - this is the Old Testament, we don't advocate that here in the Warehouse right now. One wife is enough; and one husband is enough, too. So keep that in mind.

Jacob reminds God of His promises. The Bible is full of promises. And when you know the Bible you know what your rights are. You have the privilege of laying claim to God's promise. So Jacob reminds God of His promise. He said, "You're the God who said to me, 'return to your country and I will do you good.'" But in the meantime he doesn't have any faith, because he is thinking "What am I going to do? Esau is coming with four hundred armed horsemen and we're all going to die." In the 32nd chapter and the 10th verse Jacob makes a confession. He said, "I am not worthy of the least of all the mercies, and of all the truth, which you have shown your servant. For I cross over this Jordan with my staff, and now I become two companies."

Jacob acknowledged his unworthiness. God doesn't owe us a thing; we're not worthy of anything that God gives us, we do not earn it. But God loves us anyway, and blesses us. And why, we will never know. But He acknowledges that "I am undeserving of your mercy and grace" instead of saying "God I have served you all these years, I have been faithful in all of these things and now God you owe me." He doesn't owe you anything; or me. Especially me. It's all because of His grace, His unmerited favor. And now Jacob makes a specific request in the 11th verse of Chapter 32 of Genesis. He said, "Deliver me I pray thee from the hand of my brother." He said "Deliver me." Then he sent his flocks and wives away, and then in the 16th verse, he delivered them to the hands of his servants, and said to his servants "Pass over before me and put some distance between the successive droves." Separate the company. He sent his wife and his children away, and now he is alone. He is afraid that his wives and his children are all going to be slain.

He reminds God of His promise, in the 12th verse, "I will surely treat you well and make your descendants as the sands of the sea which cannot be numbered for the multitude." What he was saying was, "God you made a promise and I can't have that many descendants if you have me killed right now and my wives and children. You promised me Lord." But you see the problem is, Jacob knew the promises but he didn't really believe them. He wouldn't have been afraid of Esau had he believed His promises.

Now he tries to make plans to win Esau over, because Esau was a long way off. Jacob decides "Here's what I am going to do, I am going to send some presents to my brother, because I know he is a business man too, and he is materialistic, and I am going to make him appreciate me." And so he sends him a gift. He sent two hundred female goats, twenty male goats, two hundred ewes, twenty rams, thirty milch camels with their calves, forty cows, ten bulls, twenty female donkeys and ten foals. This was a very lavish present that in itself at that time would have made a man wealthy. And he sent this great present out there, hoping to win Esau's favor because he knew Esau was a man of the flesh who did not believe, who had no faith in God.

Even in the New Testament, we find the difference between Esau the man of the flesh, and Jacob the man of faith. God had to change him. And he rose that night and took his two wives and the female servants and eleven sons, and he crossed over Jabbok, and he took them and sent them over the brook, and sent over what he had, and then Jacob was left alone. And a man wrestled with him until the breaking of day. This is one of the many theophany in the Old Testament; God appearing in the form of a man. He didn't wrestle with the man; the man wrestled with him. He actually wrestled with God, and God wrestled him. He named the place where this happened Peniel, which means "Face of God."

Now God is breaking down Jacob's dependence upon himself. God is wrestling his dependence upon himself, and his nimble mind, and his sleek way of maneuvering people, and charming people, and getting what he wanted. He never trusted God to really do things. He felt he had to do everything himself, even though he made this beautiful prayer. By his actions we know that he had no faith in God. No real faith. And God is showing Jacob his prayers were useless because he did not believe that God was going to do anything. All of his trust was in himself.

When you and I are facing crisis; how much do we believe God? How much do we believe His Word? And how much do we go about in our own intellect, and our own abilities, trying to solve the problems ourselves instead of trusting Him? Trying this and trying that. Jacob had reached the point when God reached out and He touched his thigh, and when He did it shrunk. The tendon in his leg, and Jacob's hip went out of joint, and he became crippled. And now he was totally dependent, and the only thing he could do is just hold on to God.

The man touched Jacob's thighs and put his hip out of socket, and Jacob could no longer wrestle. All he could do was hold on. And He said to Jacob, "Let me go." And Jacob said, "I will not let you go unless you bless me." And He said, "What is your name?" "My name is Jacob." God knew his name but He asked him his name. Jacob means supplanter or usurper, a man who seeks to take the position of someone else. There are a lot of Jacobs in the world today. You probably have some you work with, they want to get rid of you and take over. They want what you have. This was Jacob's name, because it described what he was. But now God said, "I am going to change your name to Israel." Israel means "God's fighter."

God's fighter, the man that fights for God, in union with God, the man that strives to accomplish God's purpose in his life. His name was changed because he was changed by the awesome power of the living God. He wrestled with Him but God won the battle. Jacob prevails only once he was broken, when he was helpless, and recognized how desperately he needed God. You see God doesn't work like we do. There's the story of Gideon and the Midianites, they are plundering the nation of Israel. They are stealing their crops, they are tormenting them, and he thinks well maybe we ought to get together with our conquered people and make some alliances with them and make a big army so we can go whip the Midianites. God had a different way. They defeated the army of the Midianites by having three men take earthen jars that had lamps, fire lamps in them. That's how God did it.

Jericho stood in the way, this massive wall that was impenetrable. So what did God do? He said okay, you guys walk around the walls, walk around the walls till I tell you to quit. And then you will blow your trumpets and the walls will come down. And they did. And about twelve, fifteen years ago archeologists found those crumpled walls, after saying for years they weren't there. They just didn't dig deep enough.

See, God works differently than we do. Our problem is we don't believe it sometimes, we don't accept it and we don't expect it. So when you pray, I encourage you to believe it, accept it and expect it. Trouble of it is, we resort to human ingenuity, which is such a poor substitute for God.

Jacob said to God in the 29th verse of Genesis 32, he said "Tell me your name, I pray." He said, "Why is it that you ask about my name?" And He just blessed him there. The one whom we are really dependent on is God. You just keep going, trusting God. And you find out that He's worthy of the trust. Look at your record and God's record. Don't just talk to God, or pray, but believe Him. Prayer without faith is like a boat without an oar. You ever try to paddle a row boat with your little paws, it's difficult. You trust

Him. Why? Because He is trustworthy! He's never failed you. He's never failed me. Things have not turned out like we wanted them sometimes, but they turned out the way He wants them. And if you can't see His purpose that's alright. You can't even really understand why these lights burn. Oh I am an electrical engineer, I can tell you; but you still don't have it, you still don't.

So Jacob called the name of the place Peniel, "For I have seen God face to face, and my life is preserved." And as he passed over Peniel the sun rose upon him, and he halted upon his thigh. Therefore the Children of Israel eat not of the sinew which shrank, which is upon the hollow of the thigh, unto this day: because he touched the hollow of Jacob's thigh in the sinew that shrank.

We do not overcome the challenges of life with inward struggles. I am terrible about that; Lord I know you, and trust you, and yet... And then the Lord will speak to me, "Then why are you up at two o'clock in the morning pacing the floor in your study? Where is that quiet faith?" Only after we look at all of the monsters, and all of the impossibilities, and all of challenges that seem so hopeless do we look to God.

I have learned something. My nature is to pace. One of my dearest friends told my wife one day something that wasn't very nice about me. I was all wound up as usual, pacing around and everything, and he said to Mary, "Your husband is kind of like a truck driver who took two bennies and his truck won't start."

When I stop pacing and I start praying, all the peace comes. When I stop trying to figure out how I am going to do this and that, and how this need's going to be met, and how this person is going to be helped when I have nothing to give them. I recognize the Holy Spirit says "Just take them to God, He can do what they need, He can take care of their needs. He can take care of your needs."

We don't succeed with our inward struggles, we succeed when we look up. We say, "Oh God, you are so great, you are so powerful, you are so magnificent, you are so loving, you are so kind and I don't know why but you love me so much and there's nothing going on my life that you can't take care of, just like that. Teach me to trust you." And you learn to trust Him by knowing Him better, and you know Him better by talking to Him. And that's called prayer! Talking to God. There can be other people around you, but when you truly pray it's between two people, God and us. And He hears prayer and He answers them. God will act.

Sometimes we believe God's not going to help, God's not going to change anything, everything is going to go on like it is, there is very little hope… and we just get into a real torment. The problems are real, the challenges are real, but compared to God they are nothing! In my mind my fears are the shovel digging my grave, but compared to God, they are nothing.

Ephesians 3:20 says, "Now to Him who is able to do exceedingly and abundantly above all that we think or ask according to the power that works in us." The power of the presence of God, Amen.

THE PITIFUL PRAYER

Moses

Numbers 11:11-15

If you ever have an urge to pray and to seek the Lord, that urge came from God, and it will direct you to God. As you pray you will enter into a partnership, and become one with the triple person of God - Father, Son and Holy Spirit; the three in one. What is so magnificent is that when we become one with God, God moves through us, and in us. And yet when we arise from prayer we're still the same person - our same personality, but empowered with God. God is then able to use us, because we come to that awareness that we're not alone, that God is in us. And that He has limitless power.

There were two blind men following Jesus, and Jesus said to the first "What do you want?" He said, "Lord, that I might receive my sight." Then Jesus asked the question that comes to all of us in prayer, "Do you believe that I am able to do what you are asking me to do? Do you believe it?" And Jesus said to him, "According to your faith be it unto you."

Where does faith come from? Faith comes from knowing someone. If you have faith in someone you know them. I have friends, and I have faith that when I say we'll be on time to meet together for some purpose, I know which ones will be on time, and which ones might be on time. So if it is something very, very important like a golf game, I usually tell them about ten minutes earlier than it actually is. Therefore everybody arrives on time. Of course, I have never been able to really perfect that gift here in the church, about getting everybody to meet on time. If I say that service starts at a quarter of twelve, or a quarter of whatever, then they would come at twelve. And if I say twelve fifteen, they would come at twelve thirty. And so, I have surrendered. And I'm not bitter, it's just the reality of life. Some of you just cannot be here on time, and by the grace of God you also are loved. I want you to understand that from the bottom of my heart.

Faith. Where does faith come from? Faith comes from hearing the Word of God. "Father, open our hearts to receive the Word of God and may faith grip us today, and may we come to a better understanding of prayer. We ask this in Jesus' name, Amen."

Moses is leading the Children of Israel out in the wilderness. He led them for forty years, and they were provided with food called "manna." The literal translation of the word manna is, "What is it?" And so for forty years, they ate "What is it?" And I'm sure that they got tired of it. We know that they did, because the Bible says so. In the 11th chapter of Numbers, in the 4th through the 6th verse, the Bible said, "Now, the mixed multitudes who were among them yielded to intense cravings. So the Children of Israel also wept and said, "Who will give us meat to eat? We remember the fish which we ate freely in Egypt, the cucumbers, the melons, the leaks, the onions and the garlic." I can't imagine anybody missing garlic. "But now our whole being is dried up, and there is nothing at all except manna before our eyes."

Manna, manna, manna! When you think of the miracle of God's provision; two million people out in a desert, a desolate area for forty years. Two million people to feed, two million people who daily witnessed a miracle; their clothes never wore out, their sandals never wore out, as they followed the leadership that God had given them in Moses. Taking them through this wilderness, to prepare them to accomplish the ultimate purpose He had for them, which was to return to the land of promise that God had promised them. And that out of that land would come the Messiah that would bring redemption to the whole human race. There would be a dew in the evening that would settle down, and on top of the dew, the manna would come. It was a small seed, and they would pick it up and take it into their tents in whatever containers that they had, and they would grind it up and bake it into loaves. And that would be their meat, and sustain them, and give them great health, as they walked for years through this period of wilderness.

But now they begin to cry out against God, so Moses began to hear the people complaining, and he listened to them, and they were always parading by his tent. "Moses you are a failure, look what you've done to us." In verses 10 through 15 the Word says, "Then Moses heard the people weeping throughout their families, everyone at the door of his tent, and the anger of the Lord greatly aroused. Moses also was displeased. So Moses said to the Lord," and here is his pitiful prayer. "Why have you afflicted your servant, and why have I not found favor in your sight? That you have laid the burden of all these people on me. Did I conceive all these people? Did I beget them that you should say 'carry them in your bosom as a guardian carries a nursing child' to the land which you swore to their fathers. Where am I to get meat to give them to eat? I am not able to bear all these people alone because the burden is too heavy for me. And if you treat me like this, please kill me, here and now. If I have found favor in your sight, do not let me see my wretchedness."

I have never really reached that point where I've said to God "Kill me here and now." I haven't reached that point in my life, and I haven't carried the burden of Moses. But I have been a gifted complainer, and moaner, and weeper, and accuser of God, and in spite of that He's loved me, and loves me, and uses me in any way that He sees fit. Moses' pitiful prayer, it was a prayer filled with self-pity. God, how could you let this happen to me? He began to reproach God. How am I supposed to feed all these people? Am I supposed to go to the herds that we have, that supply our milk and our cheese, and are we supposed to kill all the herds? In other words, God, it simply can't be done.

Does it remind you of the disciples, when Jesus said "All these people have been with us and they haven't had anything to eat?" And Jesus said to them go out and get what's there, and they came back with a few loaves and fishes. And they looked at it, and said in other words, "Jesus, there's just no way we can feed these people."

And they said we can't go into town and buy food, because we're out in the wilderness. And they had no faith. But Jesus just said, "Let me bless it," and they took up extra food, saved all the scraps after everybody had their fill.

Moses lost faith, and he was questioning God, and feeling put upon. Have you ever experienced that? Don't say "Yes," because it includes 100% of you. It's true, and that certainly includes me. You say "You're judging me." No, I'm just reporting the facts. There's a time that we question God; "Why aren't you helping me? Why aren't you blessing me? Why isn't this prayer answered? What's going on?" And you begin to have your faith shaken.

Moses usually prayed, majestic, magnificent prayers. He was magnificent in his faith and prayers as he stepped into the water and the seas parted. He was magnificent in his prayers when he would lift up his rod and God would conquer armies that came against him. He was magnificent in his prayers when two million people had no water out in the wilderness, and he smote the rock and out of it gushed water, a powerful spring of water that supplied two million people and all their livestock. A magnificent man of prayer. Some of his prayers are so majestic, and there were times that Moses himself was majestic; a mighty man of God. Some of the decisions and some of his writings still affect the laws that are written in nations, where wise men sit down and look at the guidance and the wisdom that came out of Moses. You look at him, and ask how could he be reduced to this point where, when the people were complaining about food, he wants God to kill him? And begins to tell God, "How could you possibly provide meat for all of these people?"

Think about him, first of all; he was miraculously spared from death. The Children of Israel had forgotten it, as they wanted to go back to Egypt, but the fact was that for that period of time, the eldest son in every family was slain as soon as he was born. Moses' mother made provision for him, and put him in a little basket woven of bulrushes and sealed with pitch. And Pharaoh's daughter took him in, and he became a prince. He became a son of pharaohs, and the leader of armies. He was a mighty and powerful man in the nation of Israel. He'd also received spiritual training from his mother, from his family, just as a little boy before he went full time into Pharaoh's house. Now he had all of these human positions and power, and he decided that he would go and liberate the Children of Israel. But he became a miserable failure. Instead of helping them, he saw an Egyptian overlord abusing one of them with a whip, and he took the man and killed him, and buried him in the sand. And he had to flee for his life.

So, for forty years, a man that was a prince became a shepherd, and he stood out in the wilderness and completely gave up. There is no record of him ever trying to go back into Egypt, or ever having a concern again for the deliverance of the People of Israel. He was a defeated, beaten man who herded sheep for his father-in-law out in the wilderness. One day God revealed Himself to him, and God showed Himself in the form of a bush that was burning, but the bush was not being consumed. And he heard the voice of God Himself say, "Take off your sandals, for the ground you are on is Holy ground." He took his sandals off, and God begins to speak to him. God said "I'm going to send you back for deliverance. I want you to go before Pharaoh and speak." And, what did Moses say? He said, "I can't do it, I stutter."

I can't, have somebody else do it. I don't want to do it. Here he is trusting in his own power now he's a disgrace, now he's lost all confidence in himself and in God. Forty years in the desert and he told God he couldn't speak and finally, when he became a leader and was leading the Children of Israel, his authority was constantly challenged. First by his brother and sister, Aaron and Mariam. God had to re-establish his spiritual leadership and authority over the nation of Israel by his sister being covered with leprosy, and then healed in response to prayer. Then there was Cora and Dothan, who caused the people to rise up against him while he was on Mount Sinai, actually speaking with God in the very presence of God. He spoke to God twice, and came down from the mountain, his face glowing with the power of God. He had such power and confidence in God that he took the tablets that He had given him, and smote them to the ground. And they were shattered. Then he had to go back with the new tablets that he was forced to quarry out.

And now here he is after all these years of miracle; water coming forth from a stone, the seas being parted, rivers being separated, nations falling before them, all of these miracles, and now he says "God, they want meat, I can't provide it. I can't stand it anymore; kill me right this minute." God said "No, I have another plan for you Moses." He took care of Cora, he took care of Dothan, and those who followed them, and the earth opened up and swallowed them. And he established his leadership. These people brought division that were crying out for meat, and in relationship to two million people it was relatively a handful of people who became so obsessed with their appetite that they said, "If I don't get meat, I don't know what I'm going to do."

I kind of experienced that when I was back at the East Coast conference. A guy came up to me that used to be on the West Coast, and he said, "How long has it been since you've been to In and Out Burger?" He began to tell me how he longed for In and Out Burgers, and oh if there was some way they could get back to the East Coast. Then he went on to say, "Tell me how they tasted." I said, "They just tasted like a hamburger." He said, "No, I'm talking about In and Out Burgers." We can actually get this kind of a craving, but it's not just for food, it's for something in our life. And we can begin to pursue something with a hunger, and a craving, that puts everything else into the background of our consciousness. We strive, we want it. It could be food, it could be a car, it could be a better house, it could be clothing, it could be position, it could be wealth, it could be anything; but suddenly a craving so takes us over that we have little consciousness or thought of God.

So the Lord said to Moses, "Gather seventy men of the elders of Israel, whom you know to be elders of the people and officers over them, and bring them to the tabernacle of meeting that they may stand there with you. And then I will come down and talk with you there, and I will take the Spirit that is upon you and will put the same upon them, and they shall bear the burden of the people with you, that you may not bear it by yourself alone." So now seventy men of God, they were called the elders.

When we think about elders in the church, people think in terms of somebody that takes care of the business or head of the business committee, or part of the business committee taking care of the earthly things of the church. But that's not what an elder is in a biblical sense. They are men and women who have been gifted, and called of God to minister. To share the Word, to lead in prayer, to go to the sick that are needy, to touch human need.

God selects the elders, and they become evident to the people without having a designation, or having a hat that says "elder" on it or having a shirt that says "elder" or "chief elder" or "minor elder" or "middle-class elder". It is simply someone that is willing, and God lays his hand on them to serve. They will always be elevated to a place of service, that's what ministry is; it's being a servant to the people of God. That's why a minister should never get the big head, and never go around with a humble strut, because the word "minister" means servant. It doesn't mean mighty man of God, of power of the hour, that stands there in his great big multi-colored photo, striking the power and the glory and the majesty of God, and telling people that "It only comes through me and without me you are nothing." So, I have a little strong feeling in that area, and I'll try not to not get carried away this morning.

So here they are, and the Spirit begins to grip them. Two of the seventy men who were anointed by God didn't make it to the tabernacle. They were out among the people prophesying, and the power of God was being exercised through their lives. One was named Eldad, and one was named Medad. Please don't put that burden on your child if it's born. But anyway Eldad and Medad, these men of God were prophesying in the court, and a young man ran up and he told Moses. He said, "Eldad and Medad were out in the camp prophesying. Stop them." In other words, "What are they doing?" Stop having them prophesy, don't let them have a ministry among the people that isn't authorized, sanitized, glorified and mesmerized.

But Moses gave this response, and we find it in the 29th verse of this chapter. "Then Moses said to them 'Are you jealous for my sake? Oh that all the Lord's people were prophets and that the Lord would put His spirit upon them, and the prayer was answered.' And he said then 'You shall say to the people, consecrate yourself, for tomorrow, you shall eat meat. And if you have wept in the hearing of the Lord saying 'Who will give us this meat to eat, for it was well with us in Egypt,' therefore the Lord will give you meat and you shall eat it. And you shall eat it not one day, not two days, not five days, but for a full month, for a full month until it comes out of your nostrils and becomes a loathsome thing to you.'"

So a great wind came from the seaside where there were great cubits of quail. And the great wind blew them in around the camp at the Children of Israel. That doesn't mean that they were stacked up four or five feet deep, which is ten homers deep, which will be several bushels deep; what it means it that they came in and they were flying about three to four feet above the ground, and the Children of Israel took sticks to knock them out of the sky. And the person that took the least amount of quail, would have filled several baskets full of quail. The scripture says, "And they gathered them and they spread them out for themselves around the camp." And for hours, they ate quail. Now quail meat is a very rich meat, and for thirty days they ate quail; you'll never find the Children of Israel asking for quail again.

My friend Jack and I, a very special occasion years ago, had the joy of going to Alaska to fish. We went twice. And the second time that we went, the outfitter in the camp that was, way back on the Bering Sea, about three and a half hours from the nearest road. He didn't have much provision for us. So every day we ate salmon, salmon. I still don't like salmon. I loved it, but for six days to eat salmon; salmon lunch, salmon supper. One day he brought meat and the rest of the days we ate salmon. Why? Because it didn't cost him anything, we caught them, he cooked them and we got sick of it. Can you imagine eating quail, nothing but quail for this period of time?

God brought judgment upon those who had been complaining and stirring the camp up. You see there were two million people, but it only takes a few malcontents in any body of people, whether it's the church, or politics, or anywhere at any gathering, to bring dissention and cause strife, and bitterness, and anger. It doesn't take many complainers to accomplish that. And God brought a judgment, and a plague came, and many of the complainers died right there.

We look at Moses, and I see him as a great man for a reason. His greatness did not come through his personality. It came through the power of prayer. This particular prayer grips my heart because it looks a lot like my prayers, and maybe yours. How many times have I said, "God, how can I do what you're asking me to do?" How can I keep going Lord? Why did you ever call me to this task? Why do I have so many needs that are paraded before me that I can't do anything with? How can I meet these needs? And how long can I keep going?" I look at this fact you know, I've been preaching sermons for years, and years, and years, and I'm amazed that anybody wants to hear them anymore. You've heard everything I know, over and over again. But once in a while God tells you something through me that you didn't know, as He tells me something through you I didn't know. Lord, how can I keep doing it?

Lord, things were so good back in Egypt. I remember the days past when there was something magnificent, exciting, going on. But the realization that I have had in my heart now for two years; this has been, and is the richest, and most powerful ministry that has ever happened in Warehouse Christian ministries, because the body of Christ is being anointed by the Spirit and being raised up to minister. There are more people ministering in this body of believers now than probably ever were in our past history. There were a lot of spectators, but few ministers.

Prayer; we're no better nor worse than Moses. I'm not saying that I'm going to accomplish what Moses did, but what I'm saying is that he was an ordinary man that was retiring and let people run over him; his sister, his brother, people within the camp.

God had to constantly prop him up. He didn't want to obey God, didn't have enough faith in God to speak for himself. He has his brother come and do it. Constantly questioning, constantly wondering, but then after prayer, the power of God would come upon this ordinary man. And he became one of the greatest, and most extraordinary, leaders in the history of the world.

You say "That's a terrible thing to say about Moses." You can say also it about Peter. Peter at the time of the crucifixion and sufferings of Christ, he denies his Savior, that he had walked with for years, and cursed, because a little girl pointed him out and he couldn't take the consequences of persecution. And yet when the Holy Spirit fell upon him he was transformed.

I was looking at 1st Corinthians 1:27. "But God has chosen the foolish things of the world to put to shame the wise, and God has chosen the weak things of the world to put to shame the things that which are mighty." Folks, God is calling us to prayer, not just once a month, but every day of our lives. To take our ordinary lives with our fears, our failures, our insecurities, our inabilities, and to anoint us, to power us by the Spirit to do extraordinary, mighty things. Not in our name, or through our strength, but because we are vessels of God. The scripture says, "Don't you know your body is the temple of the Holy Spirit, it is a place where God dwells." And God said "In the last days, I will pour out of my Spirit upon all flesh." In Acts 1:8 the Bible said, "But you shall receive power when the Holy Spirit has come upon you, and shall be witnesses to me in Jerusalem and Samaria and to the ends of the earth."

This is the promise of God, and it's not for one person that happens to be called to a specific place of leadership in the church, or a place of servant in the background of the church. It's for every believer to take whatever position that God has equipped and called and prepared them to. Whether it's taking care of God's house and keeping it clean; taking care of the babies and the nursery, changing their diapers; whether it's teaching at a Sunday school class; whether it's simply praying for the body of Christ. Whatever that gift, whatever that ministry is. Whether it's witnessing in the business community, or the social community, or in the state, or in the government, or wherever it is. There is an empowerment of the Holy Spirit for every believer. But it only comes into fruition, and can only be exercised, when prayer becomes the priority of our life.

Because it isn't us who does these things; it is God in us, and God through us. And the only way we will have the power to do more than talk about it, is to have the Spirit of God carrying out the work of the Father and the Son, through our individual lives. And the only way we can do that, is to know Him, and have fellowship with Him, and to enter into the Trinity. And let the Trinity enter into you, and work through you, and empower you to go out and to accomplish wonderful things. Whatever needs to be done, if God calls you to do it, it shall be done. For the power rests with Him.

I ask you the question the scripture asks; "Is there anything too hard for the Lord?" There's plenty too hard for me, but there's nothing too hard for the Lord. As we pray, we shall be a part of this last day ingathering. And when we talk about the last days, we're not talking about the world falling apart immediately, we're talking about the collapse of human government. And we're experiencing that all over the world right now. That's what we're talking about. And those are the days when Jesus said there will be this great last surge, and then I will call my church into my presence.

Prayer, prayer life. Do you have one? Is that important? Somebody talked to me this morning and they said, "Louis, did you know there's a football game tonight, a professional football game." And I thought yeah, I didn't know it. I don't know whether I would have called a prayer meeting tonight or not; I'd like to think I would have anyway. But no, there's nothing in my life, and nothing in our life right now, more important than prayer. It's prayer that will bring our wayward children back to Christ. It's prayer that will heal our homes. It is prayer that will enable us to hear the voice of God, and give us the faith to exercise the will of God in our lives.

THE GOD OF OPPORTUNITY

Jabez, the Poor Son
1 Chronicles 4:9-10

In 1st Chronicles, Chapter 2, verse 55 there is a mention of a city where the scribes lived with their families. The name of the city was Jabaz. I'm sure that you've read the book or heard the story of the prayer of Jabaz, but that was the man. And he was obviously a man who loved the Word of God, because the scribes were the ones who put down the scriptures, and would go out and share their teachings throughout the villages; and in 1st Chronicles Chapter 4 verses 9 and 10, it said, "And Jabaz was more honorable than his brothers and his mother called him 'Jabaz' saying 'Because I bore him in pain.' And Jabaz called God the 'God of Israel' saying, 'Oh that you would bless me indeed and enlarge my territory and your hand will be with me and that you would keep me from evil, that I may not cause pain.' So God granted him what he requested."

Let's pray. Jesus open our hearts and give us understanding of the Word of God. And may this message be applied to our individual lives as we continue, Lord, to go through your word, and to learn how to pray more effectively, more in line with your will and your desire. I pray that faith will grow in our hearts; and confidence, whatever our circumstances. For we serve a God so big, powerful, loving and wonderful, that no power of hell or heaven or earth can keep you from blessing our lives, if we'll but pray and trust in you. We ask these things in Jesus' name, Amen.

We read the short prayer of Jabaz right in the middle of the chronicle of the names of the leaders - in other words - the *Who's Who* of Israel. And as you go through 1st Chronicles you'll see

"So and so beget so and so…" for it's a list of the fathers, and the family names. For when they came into the Land of Israel, God gave each family a piece of land for their possession, and it was intended to pass down from generation to generation, without end. As we look at this we discover that Jabaz is mentioned, but his father's name is not mentioned.

His prayer seems like a selfish prayer, but it really isn't; he says "Bless me in deed, enlarge my coast," in other words expand my property, "Let your hand be with me, keep me from evil, keep me from grief." Scripture has something interesting to say in Romans Chapter 2 verses 8 through 11, "He said but to those who are self-seeking and do not obey the truth, but obey unrighteousness, there be indignation and wrath, tribulation and anguish on every soul of man who does evil, of the Jew first and also the Greeks; but glory, honor and peace to everyone who works what is good, to the Jew first and also to the Greeks, for there is no partiality with God." In other words whoever we are, whatever our backgrounds, we are going to sow what we reap in relationship to righteousness.

Now Jabaz was an interesting name, because what it really meant was sorrow and pain. You say "Well that's just referring to child birth." There's no man who can fully understand how painful that is, I just know that at the time of birth very few husbands are very popular. But the fact is, it's not referring to childbirth at all. If it was something just in relationship to pain, then every kid in the world would be named 'Jabaz' or 'Jabazette', or whatever. Because there's always pain associated with birth. But it was speaking of the condition of the family. They were living in grinding poverty. As far as we know there was no father in the home. It kind of reminds you of what's going on in our own culture. This last year, for the first time in our history there were more children born out of wedlock than were born to married couples. And there's an ache in the heart of every child whose father is absent, don't ever doubt it. There's a pain that is there, a sense of worthlessness, because they sense that early on they were rejected. And they don't even know why; they don't understand it. But it roots in their soul, and affects their life, and affects their behavior.

The father had lost the inheritance, we don't know how for sure, but somehow through something illegal or shady. And his brothers had a bad reputation; the Bible said they were not very honorable. His whole family was looked upon as being failures, and lacking integrity or worth. This is the family that Jabaz was raised in. His mother lived in such difficulty that she named him sorrow and pain, not because of childbirth but because of the circumstance of their life, and the hopelessness of ever seeing anything change.

I was in Folsom, at the Whole Earth store the other night, getting some supper to take home, and I started talking to the young man who was a waiter. He seemed like a really neat kid, young guy, and I said, "Well how are things going?" He said, "Well I'm just grateful to have a job." I read a few weeks ago, a statistic that young people from 16 to 27, almost 50% of them are without jobs in our culture right now. We talk about how good things are going, unemployment is down to a mere 8.3%, but the economists tell us the truth is there are over two million Americans that have given up looking for work. They've sought for years to get a job. There are some of you that have gone a year, two years looking for some kind of permanent gainful employment. This is the challenge that we have.

And I started talking to this young man, it was kind of quiet, and then I said, "I really appreciate somebody saying how much they appreciate having a job". He said, "Look, I just graduated with my Master's degree. But there's no work. Everything that I've trained for...there's no place to go. At this point at least I'm working." I say, "I'm going to pray God will bless you and open a door of opportunity to you." But there are millions of people in this country right now who are on the brink of poverty; they don't have enough. And the reality is, that 15% of Americans are without work today when you take the honest number. We'll never get that from politics; but 15%. We're certainly not in the condition that Jabaz was in ancient Israel, because there was no help from the government at that period of time.

But they'd lost their land, a family with a bad reputation, and Jabaz was the exception. Sometimes we look at the challenges of life and we say "How can there be any change, how can we break this pattern of failure, this pattern of need; what can we do to change things in our lives?" Somebody says "Well, you need to go read a self-help book." But I don't think we need more knowledge, I think we need a guide. We need someone to direct us. You can go to a city and people give you directions. I even had my GPS fail me miserably the other day. It led me to a place that doesn't exist. I was in no man's land, in Dallas... It was just an empty lot in the middle of empty warehouses. I had the address right, and everything else, and when I did get there it was the right address. But the GPS had an evil spirit enter into it, and it led me into a dead-end road. What we really need is a reliable guide, someone to direct us.

Scripture tells us in Philippians 3:15, "He said, Let us therefore, as many as be perfect, be thus minded: and if in any are otherwise minded, God shall reveal even this unto you." In other words if you trust God, whenever you need guidance and direction in your life, God will reveal it to you.

Now Jabaz's Prayer is fascinating; he said "I want you Lord to keep me from evil, that it might not hurt me." He said "I want you to enlarge my borders." I want to have an understanding of what's going on, I need more property, I need more land, I need more hope. What he meant was, "When you bless me, and guide me into a place of deliverance, I want you to keep me from falling back, from doing wrong." Here he is born of a hapless mother, in poverty, no hope of a better future, terrible family circumstances, but his mother in her poverty and in her need absolutely taught him about God; because when he prayed, he knew who to pray to.

He prayed to the God of Israel, the God that had made promises and commitment to them. He prayed to the God who had promised to guide His children through the wilderness and to lead them to a place of comfort, a place where they would have plenty to eat and a land that was their own. And so Jabaz called him the "God of Israel," the God who had promised to guide them - and did guide them - through the wilderness. And Jabaz knew this because his mother taught and directed him.

And he called on the God of Israel saying, "Oh that you would bless me indeed, enlarge my territory, give me an opportunity, and that your hand would be with me and that you would keep me from evil that I may not cause pain." So he had this powerful prayer. It wasn't a selfish prayer. You look at the Lord's Prayer. I was looking at Mathew 6 Chapter 6 verse 11 through 13, as we pray in the Lord's Prayer, and it says "Give us this day our daily bread." That's not selfish. You need something to eat, folks, you've got to eat. Some of us would last a lot longer than others if there was no food, but the fact of the matter is eventually we all need to eat.

And forgive us our debts; get our credit cards paid up Lord, and deliver us from using them again, and do not lead us into temptation Lord. Don't tempt us, we're weak, but deliver us from the evil one, for yours is the kingdom, the power and the glory forever.

So Lord enlarge my borders, restore to me what was lost by my family. Lord I'm not satisfied to live like this. I don't want a bad reputation, I want to be an honorable person, I want to glorify you, I want my life to have meaning. In other words, Lord, give me an opportunity to get out of where I'm at, and lead me to a place of victory. Provide for my material needs, Lord, as well as my spiritual. Give me an opportunity. And when it's there, Lord, help me to find it. Let me see what it is. And God will answer your prayer. He always does. God will direct you.

We've spoken before about Tim Tebow, brother Tebow. I prayed for him, because you know the enemy just loves to bring him down. He was being interviewed, and was asked a question suggesting how he didn't have any chance of being successful at his calling of being a professional footballer player. And they said, "Well, what's going to happen if next year you lose everything, and they cut you and get rid of you? What about the future?" It wasn't a nice sweet question that was asked to this young man. I'm sure you know the loving, beautiful spirit that's in so many of these sportscasters. But he answered "Well, I don't know the future, but I know who holds my future. And if I win, He's there. And if I lose, He's there." And that's what we need to learn.

Your future is not in the hands of the economy, or the political circumstances of our culture. Your future cannot be kept from you by man, or the Devil, or your birth, or the family that you live in, or the circumstances, whether it's poverty or wealth. Nothing can keep you from having what God wants you to have, if you will pray and seek His face, and have faith, and say "Lord give me the ability to see the opportunity that you present to me, and bless it, with your presence and with your Spirit. Let your hand be with me Lord, I don't want to do anything without you."

I've reached the point in life - and it comes and goes - sometimes I take things back, and think I can handle them better than God; and find out sure enough I still can't. So I give it right back to God. It's in pretty bad shape when I give it back to Him, but I give to back to Him anyway. And it doesn't bother God, because He can take care of anything. I've come to the point where I don't want to do anything, or say anything, that God doesn't want me to say. I don't want to do anything God doesn't want me to do, and I don't want to fail to do anything that God wants me to do. Because He's my guide. He is the one who will lead me. It isn't some program that will lead you out of poverty, or lead you out of need, or lead you to a place of spiritual, emotional, or physical healing; it is God Himself. It is God's presence that will give you these opportunities. Let your hand be with me Lord, I don't want to do anything that you won't participate in.

God won't participate in anything illegal, dishonest, destructive. He won't participate in adultery, fornication, any cheating, any lying, any stealing. God doesn't share in that. Lord don't let me get involved in anything where you can't be in the middle. Lord I want to be one step behind you every day that I walk. Be my guide, be my director, deliver me from my pessimism. Deliver me from my fear of the future. I don't know what the future holds, but I know you hold the future. Lord, I know that you love me, and I know that you care about me, and I know that you have the power to do anything that needs to be done in my life.

We don't need knowledge, we need a guide. And we find that guide when we pray. Prayer; what is prayer? We talked about that a few weeks ago when Adam and Eve uttered the first prayer in the scripture; it is very simply, conversation with God. Just talk to God. You don't have to pray in Elizabethan English to be holy. God can understand "the" as well as "thee". You just talk to God. "Lord, I'm confused;" the Lord will say, "I know." "Lord I don't have any direction;" the Lord will say; "I know." "But you do, Lord." And He says, "I know." "So guide me."

Most prayers in my life are answered in such a quiet way, that I hardly recognize the prayer has been answered until I start thinking about it. I seldom get goose bumps and tingles, my hair seldom stands on edge. I just look back and I say "Wait a minute, God; I prayed about that and so this is how you've done it. This is the door that you've opened, this is how you direct me." Lord, I just want to be in tune with you so I can hear you, and so here Jabaz is praying. Now he has an awareness of his past, and of his family inclinations. And we all have to be conscious of that; that's why he said "Lord, keep me from evil that it might not hurt me;" in other words, don't let my human tendencies - that are away from you - hurt me, and destroy what you've given me.

Lord, I've had a bad temper all my life; don't let me fly off the handle anymore, and say things that are harmful and destructive. Lord, I live in a culture that is obsessed with pornography and unholy sexual desires; Lord, keep me away from being obsessed with sex. Lord, we live in a culture that many times is greedy; don't let me get into greed. And Lord, when you bless me, don't let me be lifted up in arrogance, as though it was something that I did because I'm smarter, more disciplined, or better than other people, therefore I've received all of these extra blessings. I've seen that happen to so many young men, and women. They started out faithful to God, and then God raises them up and blesses them, and they begin to forget the source of the blessing, and they turn away from God. They begin to feel, "I did it, my way not God's way." And their lives become empty and hollow, and they begin to live for themselves and not for God.

There's a warning in 1st Timothy Chapter 6 and verse 10, "For the love of money is the root of all kinds of evil, for which some have strayed from the faith, and in their greediness have pierced themselves through with many sorrows." Jabaz was aware of his human weakness, of the proclivities of his family. He was aware of the challenges that would face him as God blessed him and prospered him. But here's what he did - and we mentioned it at the beginning of the message this morning. Jabaz recovered the land. You see, in the nation of Israel, because God was the government, people always got a second chance. Every fifty years there would be the Year of Jubilee. In the middle of the fiftieth year, at the tenth day of the seventh month, they weren't to plant any more crops. The land was to have a year of rest. And every slave and bond servant was to be freed. And if you'd lost your property or land for whatever circumstance, that land would be restored to you; or the nearest living relative if you were not there for it to be restored. It was the Year of Jubilee; everything was restored, you started over.

God blessed Jabez, and when it came time to have his land restored he had the price to pay. He restored his land, and he created a city, and in that city he made a special place for those scribes; the men who lived to study and share the Word of God. So God kept him from evil, God directed him, and the scribes and their families had a place of safety, and security, and provision in which to live. Because this one young man, in the most difficult circumstances imaginable, who had no hope, a mother so filled with the pain and sorrow of hopelessness and grinding poverty that she called him 'sorrow' or 'pain', prayed to God for guidance. The circumstances that he was born into were hopeless, but with God all things are possible, and your past doesn't make any difference whatsoever. Because God said "I will create and make everything new as you walk with me." I will open doors of opportunity, and I will bless you, and I will give you all you need materially; and then you in turn will honor me and give back to me, and glorify me, that the cycle of blessing might continue from person to person, from generation to generation. And that's what Jabaz is all about.

KING ASA'S PRAYER

Righteous Reform
2 Chronicles 14-16

Today we are going to talk about Asa's prayer, one of the greatest short prayers that you will ever read. So full of meaning, and of directions for our own lives and our prayer life.

Asa was a young man when he took the throne. The grandson of Solomon, he was the third king of the nation of Judah, when the two tribes of Judah and Benjamin separated from the ten tribes of Israel. He commanded Judah to seek the Lord, God of their fathers, for they had turned away from God. All the miracles of God's provision, all their history was put aside and they began to follow false gods, the gods of the peoples around them. They set up idols, and when you go back and look at the Hebrew word, most of the idols were obscene. The word that we would use is pornography. Their worship was filled with violence and sexual immorality. When worshiping Baal, the great brazen god with arms out stretched, they would put fire inside the idol and make it white hot, then lay their newborn babies on those white hot arms of that giant god and watch them die as they went into their sexual orgies.

God in his mercy would give them time to repent, and from time to time they did repent. But then they would have another wicked king who set the standard for the nation, and they would go away from God once again. Then God raised up this young man Asa as king. Second Chronicles Chapter 14, we'll share with you verses 2 through 5. "Asa did what was good and right in the eyes of the Lord his God. For he removed the altars of the foreign gods in the high places. And he brake down the images, and cut down the groves, and commanded Judah to seek the Lord God of their fathers, and to do the law and the commandments. Also he took away out of all the cities of Judah the high places and the images; and the kingdom was quiet before him."

We can say that Asa went into the nation of Judah and started a moral revolution. To have something similar in this country we would suddenly have to restore the teachings of the Bible - which this nation was founded on - back into the courts, into the schools, into our daily lives. We would have to have leaders who would close all the porn parlors, shut down prostitution and drug dealing; completely enforce righteousness. They say you can't change people's hearts that way; no you can't, but you can certainly suppress the public display and growth of evil.

We do that already in our culture. We do it through public shame. It wasn't long ago that the greatest athletes were admired; but now if they achieve great records we begin to suspect they are on steroids. And so there is a public disfavor upon those who have used steroids. There are other activities that we are concerned about, that we reject and encourage people to turn them away from. It wasn't long ago, and you would see it in some of the old black and white movies, there was a lot of smoking. You don't see so much in the movies now. People don't smoke much in public because it has become socially unacceptable. If you want to smoke freely and be socially accepted you must go to Europe. So, there is a public consciousness that affects our behavior.

Now we have laws that teachers must teach moral principles that they do not believe in, and that the Bible does not accept. And we also have laws that say you must keep God and the Word of God out of the public arena. We started this nation with prayer and were blessed because Christ was our Lord, and He was the ruler of this nation. Though we committed a multitude of sins, still the Word of God guided our leaders. Many of the leaders who founded and signed the Declaration of Independence were ordained ministers.

But now in the public arena, from entertainment to universities, they mock God and mock Jesus. You see the change. But

Asa brought back consciousness of the greatness of God, and he enforced His righteousness. Then, to make it take, he had to change the hearts of people. Years ago I went over to the house of a friend of mine. He and his wife, they invited me in, and I looked over, and I just love their kid, he is a cute little guy called Brandon. He was sitting in a corner. I said, "Oh, he did something wrong?" They said, "He must have, but we can't figure out what it was. He just took his chair and went over to the corner and sat there, and said he had to have time out for ten minutes. We've been looking all over the house to see what happened."

So you can't enforce righteousness, but the nation that honors God will be honored by God. It can't be legislated as far as the heart is concerned, but we can create public shame. Asa did something that was remarkable at a time of peace, it's there in the 14th chapter of 2 Chronicles verses 6 through 8. He began to build and fortify the cities. This was amazing, because there was no war during that time, because the Lord had given them rest. So Asa said, "Let us build these cities up, make walls around them and towers and gates and bars while the land is yet before us, when we're in peace because we have sought the Lord our God. We have sought him and He has given us rest on every side." So they built and prospered. And Asa had an army of 300,000 from Judah who carried shields and spears, and from Benjamin, 280,000 men who carried shields and drew bows, and all these were mighty men of valor. This little nation, this tiny nation that was less than half the size of California, had a standing army of 580,000 soldiers.

It was only a couple of decades ago when our standing army in this country was only about 700,000. Now our standing army is one million, four hundred and twenty six thousand, seven hundred and thirteen... thereabout. But look at the size of this nation, and the size of Judah. Asa recognized they were going to soon need that army. Because no matter how smooth things are going in our life there will come a time, I promise you I don't like it, but everything will change. You have plenty of money, everything is going good, you're in good health, then something happens and bam! Your whole world changes. That's life.

Here they have this army, but you look in the 9th and the 10th verse of Chapter 14 in 2 Chronicles, then Zerah the Ethiopian came out against them with an army of one million men. They've only got 580,000 and now there's a million men coming with three hundred chariots. The chariots were the equivalent of today's tanks. They would have blades on the wheels and they would have all sorts of weapons to drag that would just mow people down, and they would charge with these three hundred armed chariots, armored plates and horses, and they would just wreak havoc on the troops that were lined up against them. The scripture said that Zerah the Ethiopian wanted to conquer the world, and Judah was his first stop.

Think of how many supplies, how many animals, how much food they had to have to take care of a million men. Now they are marching down against this tiny little nation of Judah. And suddenly the 580,000 man army didn't seem too good, because now they were outnumbered almost two to one. Nor did Judah have chariots. And so, faced with this threat, what does Asa do? He finds time to pray! This is remarkable, this is wonderful; he went to prayer.

The scripture teaches us a great deal about facing challenges, and how we face them, in the New Testament. First Corinthians 10:11 said, "Now all of these things happen to them as examples and they were written for our admonitions upon whom the ends of the ages have come." In other words, God sent us the Old Testament to give us examples of how He works, and how He delivers in the lives of men. So when we study the Old Testament, every story is an example with something in there for us to specifically learn. Asa's prayer was a beautiful prayer, although it's only one verse - the 11th verse of Chapter 14 of 2 Chronicles. I'm sure the prayer was much longer than that, because he had a million men facing him, but it boiled down to this. Asa cried out to the Lord his God and said "Lord it is nothing for you to help whether with many or with those with no power. Help us oh Lord our God for we rest on you, and in your name we go against this multitude oh Lord. You are our God, do not let man prevail against you."

Here's something remarkable about Asa's prayer; he didn't instruct God. Usually when I pray I give God a list. "Lord; here are some ways you can answer my prayer." My mind kind of triggers that way, and I put a whole list. And it seems like every time I do that God puts another box on my list that says, "None of the above." And He always checks it. You see, when you begin to pray don't limit God to one specific thing. God can answer prayers in a multitude of ways, but He will answer when you pray. Now be really honest in your heart; how much time do you daily spend in prayer? Don't tell anybody because you might have one minute more than they do and you would have pride to deal with, so don't tell anybody how much you pray.

Help us oh God, we have no power. God I can't do anything, only you can conquer this army that's come to destroy us and take your people into captivity. And Lord, you said that we're your people and we know that we are, so don't let anybody shame you Lord. Do it however you want Lord, but do it. They go along, like I said everything is fine and then suddenly there's a million man army out there in front of you. You say, "That's not true;" well it's seems like it if it's just you. You're faced with real challenges and real problems in our world, in our lives, they suddenly rise up.

One of our brothers came and we talked and prayed recently. He was going along and everything seemed fine, and he went in and they took x-rays and they found some growth or some problems, and they thought it might be cancer. Thank God he was delivered from it, but it changed him. And sometimes you are not delivered from it. And your life changes. A guy talked to me a few months ago, and he said "I thought everything was fine at home, I loved my wife, I thought she loved me, and finally she just said, 'I can't take it anymore' and she left. I had no idea, no idea." So his life changed.

Then suddenly after years of peace Asa was faced with this terrible problem, and all the odds were now against him. And the problem was too big for Asa, but it was never too big for God. There is nothing in this world that is too big for God. God has the unique ability to help us. Think about it. Joshua was facing an army that he had no chance against; what happened? God sent a storm, a giant hail storm and destroyed that army. What about Samson? He was faced with the massive army of the Philistines, there was nothing around, he looked down and there was a jawbone of a donkey. He picked it up, went out and he defeated the army with a jawbone of a donkey. God uses different things at different times. Gideon was faced with a huge army, yet God had him wheedle his troops down till they were only three hundred, and they defeated them by putting torches in jars and created a deception that caused the enemy to flee.

You see, don't limit God on how He works. You say, "Well how does God work?" Different ways at different times. What about Jonathan, King Saul's son who was a righteous man. He and his armor bearer went out, there was the army of the Philistines coming against him, they came over the brow of the hill and right there in front of them were a hundred men who were mocking God of their enemies. And Jonathan looked over to his armor bearer, and the armor bearer had to go with him. I don't know how the armor bearer felt about it but Jonathan said, "There is no restraint on the Lord to save by many or by few." He said "I don't know what's going to happen but let's go up and fight them. Just the two of us, fight one hundred. And if God wants to deliver us He will." The armor bearer must have said, "Oh man, I wish I had somebody else to bear their armor…. This guy's kind of off the reservation." And suddenly off they go … and they won. Because God went before them.

It doesn't matter to God how big our problems are because He is God. And God has no big problems. You say, "What about all of the sins and wickedness that goes on in the world." Well God said, "I'm going to let it go until the cup of my wrath is filled to the brim and begins to spill over." And I look at the wickedness of the world that we live in and the horrible things that take place, the terrible things that are done to children, people, and I wonder when that next drop of wickedness is going to cause the cup of wrath to spill over, and the judgment of God to come as He takes His church out of the world. I don't know. He can deliver.

King Asa had a beautiful prayer. He asked God for specific aid. When you pray make your prayers specific. "Lord, this is from my heart, ... I need your answer, I need your direction. I need your help." He said, "Help us oh God for we rely on you and in your name we have come against these multitudes." He leaves it up to God, he said, "Lord our trust is not in ourselves, our trust is in you." The scripture talks to us about that. It says in Romans 8:31, "What then shall we say to these things? If God be for us who can be against us?" If God is for us, what difference does it make who is against us? Because anybody that's against God they already lose, they just don't know it.

God's already won the battle, God's already accomplished his work. In Hebrews 13:5, the scripture says, "Let your conduct be without covetousness, be content with such things as you have for He Himself has said 'I will never leave you or forsake you.'" And God will not leave you. He will not forsake you. He will not let you be destroyed. You will go through trials but the key word is you will go *through* the trials. I know if you are in the middle of one now, you say, "I am in an eternal trial," but it won't last. God will take you through the trial, and you will get out of the trial so you can go into another trial, and He will take you through that one. That's how the Christian life is, and it gets exciting; instead of depressing it gets exciting.

This is what God does. Asa doesn't instruct him, he seeks His face. He was going to fight but he knew that unless God helped him he would be defeated. Asa's trust was not in his army but it was in God. We're God's children, He invites us to come to Him. Hebrews 4 tells us, "Let us therefore come boldly to the throne of grace that we might obtain mercy and find grace to help us in the time of need." I don't care how big your problems are or my problems are, you begin to pray and God will help you. He will find grace in your time of need, and there's nothing too hard for the Lord. Second Chronicles 14:12, "So the Lord struck the Ethiopians before Asa and Judah and the Ethiopians fled." God gave Judah a complete victory. For the Bible said, "Asa and the people who are with him pursued to Gerar," so the Ethiopians were overthrown and they could not recover. They were broken before the Lord and His army who carried away much spoils. Think of all the equipment and the food and the animals it took to support a million people. And they took all of that back to Judah. Instead of the war destroying them they were enriched, because God had gone before them and accomplished His victory through them.

God working through and with men, that's what so exciting. When you do something, and you walk through life and you look back and say, "God was with me, God helped me." You say, "Why does God want us to do something?" Well it's kind of like a little kid; you get a big bucket of water and a little kid wants to help you. He really gets in the way, he puts his little hand on the bucket and he kind of carries it along. If you're painting, he wants to help you; that's why sometimes your pants are covered with paint from the knee down when the little kid helps. And that's kind of the way God is. He says, "I don't want you to just step aside and do nothing. But I will tell you what I'll do. I will carry the heavy end of the load. I will walk you to victory if you will trust in me. If you will trust in me."

Now the spirit of God came upon Azariah the son of Oded, this is a Prophet, Chapter 15 verses 1 and 2. And he went to meet Asa and he said to him, "Hear me Asa and all Judah and Benjamin; the Lord is with you while you are with Him. If you seek Him, He will be found, but if you forsake Him, He will forsake you." Now, it's not really a good translation. It's not that God forsakes you, but what happens is things get good and we forget God. Things improve and we start trusting in ourselves again.

And when Asa heard these words and the prophecy of Oded the prophet, he took courage and removed the abominable idols from the land of Judah and Benjamin, and from the cities which he had taken, the mountains of Ephraim, and he restored the altar of the Lord that was before the vestibule of the Lord. And they had thirty years of peace.

Now here's a sad story about us as human beings. After thirty years of God's peace and deliverance suddenly Israel rises up against Judah. The King of Israel begins to build up fortresses and getting ready to come in and try to conquer the land of Judah. But after thirty years of peace and success something happened to Asa and his walk with God. Something tragic. He didn't seek God. He became filled with pride and he began to take the success that God had granted the nation upon himself, and feel like he did it. And so with his clever mind, he said "How can I defeat Israel. I don't have the army for it, they are bigger than we are." So he went over to the King of Syria and he said to King Ben-hadad, he said, "I want you to make an alliance with me. You have a peace treaty with Israel. I want you to break that treaty and I am going to give you something." So he went into the house of God, into the Temple of God, and he took the gold and the silver and the treasures, and gave them to the King of Syria, so he would come against Israel. And it worked. They drove Israel off, but Asa didn't seek God. He bought the loyalty of the King of Syria and he brought Syria in to help him. He is not trusting God now. Thirty years of peace and blessings and prosperity, and now he has taken God's glory and God's honor and heaped it upon himself.

"I don't need God anymore." He didn't say it out loud but by his actions, he said, "I don't need you anymore Lord." I've seen God bless people and raise them up and prosper them and give them influence and power, and all of a sudden after being faithful to God, now God is in the rear view mirror of their life. So the prophet Hanani, the Seer came to Asa, King of Judah and said, "Because you have relied on the King of Syria and have not relied on the Lord your God, therefore the army of the King of Syria has escaped from your hands. Had you obeyed God, Syria would have been defeated and you wouldn't have an enemy that you bribed over there on your border." And in the thirty ninth year of his reign Asa became diseased in his feet, and his malady was severe. Yet in his disease he did not seek the Lord, but the physicians. And he developed a foot disease that later led to his death.

Who do we count on for success? You remember thirty years earlier when another prophet came to him, he honored the prophet and he honored God and he praised God. But this time the scripture said, he took the prophet who told him the truth and threw him in prison and became angry. The Hebrew word stands for 'fierce,' towards this man. He became so angry that he threw him in jail, and the Bible says he began to oppress some of his own people. And here he has a disease of the feet, it eventually destroyed his life and he never did see God again. He never called out to God for healing, for help, or for deliverance. His diseased feet are a symbol of what happens to us when our walk becomes polluted. When our daily walk is not constantly taking us toward God we go away from God towards self, toward the world and toward the devil. Be careful where you walk.

When Christ went to His disciples, He didn't wash their bodies, they'd already been washed by their quick repentance and forgiveness of their sins. But he washed their feet that their walk with God would be purified and holy, and that the pollution of sin would not ruin their lives. God desires to bless you, God desires to meet your needs, God desires to reveal Himself and His glory and power to help us as individuals and to help His church; but we have to listen to Him. And we have to spend time with Him where we can hear His voice. Instead of seeking answers everywhere else but prayer; start with prayer. It will save you a lot of bumps and bruises because things change. Things change, but God is always the same.

DANIEL'S PRAYER FOR UNDERSTANDING

Bible Prophecy
Daniel 9:1-3

There is a purpose in prayer, and God has laid out a pattern of how to pray in the Word of God. As we've been talking about recently, prayer is conversation with God. Our nation is in desperate need of prayer. If there is not a national repentance, God will get our attention in a way that none of us want. You say, "Does God bring harsh judgment?" Not at this point, no. He simply lifts His hand of blessings from us. In many areas of our government, in the education system, in the media and the culture at large, there are many people in leadership, people of influence who are trying to pry the fingers of Christ off of this nation, until His name cannot even be mentioned anymore. Laws are being passed to violate the conscience, the convictions that Christians live by. And the day may come when there will be prosecutions - even in this country that was founded on the teachings and the principles of Jesus Christ, and on the Word of God. Our nation needs prayer, and we need prayer.

This morning we're going to talk about Daniel's prayer for understanding. So let's pray that God will open our hearts to receive the Word this morning. Father, thank you for the love of Jesus, for the truth of the Word. Speak to our hearts today. Challenge us Lord, and draw us closer to Jesus. And anything that stands between us Lord, I pray that you will reveal it to us, that we might repent of our sins. Receive your forgiveness and have full fellowship with our Maker and our Lord and Savior restored, in Jesus' name, Amen.

Daniel is one of the few people in the Bible, other than Jesus, where not a single sin was recorded to his name in scripture. Daniel was plainly a very righteous person; we know that he sinned, because the Bible said all have sinned. But Daniel was an extremely righteous man who loved God, and sought to serve God in every way in his life. When Daniel was a young man he was one of the princes of Israel, a man with a brilliant mind, a devotion to God, and a love for God. Yet Israel so turned against God, and sinned again and again, that God said there was no remedy. He sent Nebuchadnezzar down to conquer the nation and to take them into captivity. Daniel was taken to the Royal palace to serve the King of Babylon.

Daniel actually ended up serving more or less as a prime minister, or one of the chief members of state, for three different kings. At the time this prophecy and this scripture was written, he was about ninety years old, still a man of influence, and spiritual power with God, and respected by all. He had three companions with him. We know their Babylonian names as Shadrach, Meshach and Abednego.

Daniel wanted to understand what was happening in the world in relationship to Israel, and what was going to happen in the future. He was praying for God to give him understanding of the writings of the prophets, in this instance specifically the prophet Jeremiah, as he was reading Jeremiah's prophecies. We pick up on Daniel Chapter 9 in verses 1 to 3, "In the first year of Darius, the son of Ahasuerus, of the seed of the Medes, which was made king over the realm of the Chaldeans." Through Jeremiah, Daniel understood from the books that the Lord would keep Jerusalem in desolation for seventy years.

Remember Israel had been driven from Jerusalem, and Jerusalem was now a ghost town, a shattered city, the Temple destroyed, the people of Israel in captivity. There were only a few left behind, primarily those of Samaritan or mixed races. Daniel recognizes that God had said Israel would remain in captivity for seventy years, and then go back to Jerusalem to rebuild the Temple and to be restored to the favor and to the blessing of God.

I was looking at the scripture that Daniel was focused on – it's found in Jeremiah Chapter 29 verses 10 and 11. "For thus said the Lord, that seventy years be accomplished in Babylon I will visit you and perform my good word toward you, in causing you to return to this place. For I know the thoughts I think toward you, saith the Lord, thoughts of peace, and not of evil, to give you an expected end."

So God said, I have plans for you; I am going to give you a future, you're not going to be slaves, you're not going to be captive any longer. God announces in advance what he intends to do. He said "I am going to bring a blessing and a hope into your life." But the problem was the Children of Israel had assimilated into the culture of the Babylonians. When they were in Israel they were keepers of sheep, now they were in Babylon they were keepers of shops. They were the merchants; they had a much easier life, a much more materially and physically pleasant and easy life to live in Babylon. And not many of them wanted to go back to Jerusalem, which was a city that was destroyed and was in ruins.

We look at the scripture. God announces what He is going to do, and He brings it about through prayer. God brings about what He intends to do through prayer. That's why our prayers are often delayed in being answered, because we have not prayed enough to receive what God has promised. It is God who has the plan. It is God who will do it. But He has asked us, and required us, to enter into prayer to bring it to fruition. One author said, "Prayer was not given to make God work for us, but prayer is God's way of involving us in what He intends to do." God intended to bring the Children of Israel back to Jerusalem, but He wanted to involve them. And Daniel studying the scripture recognized that the time was almost up for their captivity. It was almost time for them to go back. And of course, under King Zerubbabel and Ezra and Nehemiah, they did in fact go back, and begin to restore the walls of the city, and to restore and rebuild the Temple in Jerusalem.

God delays what He intends to do when we fail to pray. What did God say He was going to do for these folks? He said I have not evil for you, but I have good things for you. I have hope for you, and He said I am going to bless you. But you're not going to receive that hope and that blessing until you begin to pray. In James Chapter 4 verses 2 and 3, the Bible talks about prayer. He said, "You lust and do not have; you murder and covet yet cannot obtain; you fight and war; yet you do not have because you do not ask." There are some times God wants to bless you, but you are not asking Him. I should say "Us" because there are many times that I am not as faithful in prayer, and not mindful of the promises of God. I get all worried and upset and distressed, then I begin to get into the Word, and read the promises of God, and peace is restored to my life. I know that God never intends evil, or wrong, or bad for us, He always intends good. But it's through prayer that I find that blessing. And it is through prayer that God comes down and intervenes in the circumstances of our lives.

If we want to go on without praying, God lets us. But His purpose and His will is to bless us, and give us hope. And that blessing and hope come when we begin by faith to pray, and to claim the hope that God has given us. James said "You do not have because you do not ask, and you do not ask or receive because you ask amiss, that you may spend it upon your pleasures."

When I was a young guy I had a friend, and he was so desperate to enter into an immoral life that he actually prayed that God would send somebody into his life that he could have fornication. That's a prayer God doesn't answer. The Devil will help you with that. He will put you in bondage to the lust of the flesh, the lust of the eye, and the pride of life, if you turn away from God. Your life is going to be filled with something - either good or evil - and the choice is yours. God has already said that His desire is to bless you, and to give you hope, and to give you a future. But it is up to us to lay hold by faith, prayer, and obedience, to what God has for us.

So Daniel's great prayer begins. He said, "I pray to the Lord my God and make confession and say 'Oh Lord, great and awesome God who keeps his covenant, and has mercy for those who love Him and with those who keep His commandments.'" For God said, "I will keep my covenant and my promises with you if you love me and if you keep my commandments." But when we live in willful, habitual rebellion against God, and we live in willful, habitual sin against God; then the blessings are not going to come. And the peace of God is not going to come. And the favor of God is not going to come. And the protection of God will be lifted from our lives.

Jesus prayed for us, and He taught us how to pray. He said that when we start to pray, we acknowledge the greatness, the power, and the sovereignty of God. We start off in Matthew 6:9, prayers we're all familiar with, "Our Father Who Art In Heaven." We acknowledge that God is the Creator, that He is in the heavens, that He fills the universe with His presence and spirit. He is all powerful, all knowing. He is righteous; everything He does is right, nothing God does is wrong. And everything has a purpose that He has predetermined in the lives of people, and in the lives of the nations of the world. "Our Father who art in heaven, hallowed be thy name." You are a great, and a terrible, and a mighty God, not someone to be trifled with or treated in a casual way. A God to be honored and come before in humility and awe, to seek His face. "Thy kingdom come. Thy will be done on earth as it is in heaven." That's how Christians pray. "Lord, not my will, but your will be done." It is better if you choose for me because you know the future. You know the present and not only that Lord, you know me so much better than I know myself."

I don't know myself as well as I would like, but God knows me, and God knows every part of my life and your life. God knows everything that's going on in your mind, and in your spirit. You see, many times our sins, they're not overt, but covert. Hidden. Only we know what they are, the stuff that we harbor in our mind, the Godless passions and desires that we play host to, sometimes willingly. We put ourselves in situations where we know we're going to be tempted to sin, tempted to do that which is displeasing to God. God knows all of those things, and He loves us, and He is the one who will guide us in our prayer life. But we must pray. We must pray.

Daniel focused on the nature of God. He said "God you are great and a terrible God." There is no power on earth that can resist you; there is no human being that can withstand you. He said, "You have sovereign power over the nations of the earth." We're praying for these nations, but God will decide who He raises up in leadership and who He puts down. And many times the leadership we have reflects our righteousness or our sinfulness, God is giving us what we deserve. And the thing that I pray most for in this nation, is that God does not give us what we deserve; but He will give us what His grace permits.

We look around, we see people in bondage to the lust of the flesh, destroying marriages, breaking faith with the wife or the husband that God has placed in their life, going from one person to another. Or they've become "without natural affection, trucebreakers, false accusers, incontinent, fierce, despisers of those that are good."

But the Bible said that God has the sovereign power over the nations of the earth. And the prayer that I pray continually is "God, please don't give us what we deserve, but give us grace, and forgiveness." Bring a revival, bring us back to God. Lord, don't let us continue on a path where 50% of the babies born in 2011 were born out of wedlock. It places an enormous burden upon the mothers, upon the families, and it places a terrible load upon the children. It drastically increases the probability of poverty, and need, and want.

So Daniel prayed, "Help us to keep your commandments." He sees God as awesome and majestic, but Daniel also sees that God is a God of infinite tender love, and compassion. God hates sin because of what it does to His children. He hates what it does in our lives, the scars, the wounds that we inflict upon ourselves, and others inflict upon us. God hates sin, but He loves us. That's why God wants to free us from the power and the bondage of sin; because He loves us.

Daniel confesses his sin. In the 6th verse of Daniel 9, he said, "Neither have they hearkened unto thy servants the prophets, which spake in thy name to our kings, our princes, and our fathers, and to all the people of the land." He said we've not listened to those who teach and preach the Word of God, you know, we just don't accept it. We listen a little bit, pass it on if they say something that challenges us, or makes us uncomfortable. Then we just quit going to church. He said we've sinned, we've done wrong, we've acted wickedly, we've rebelled. We have turned aside from His commandments and His ordinances, neither have we heard His servants the prophets. We've ignored the truth, and the Word of God.

We've not sought the favor of the Lord, he said. In the 13th verse he prays, "As it is written in the Law of Moses, all this evil is come upon us: yet made we not our prayer before the Lord, that we might turn from our iniquities, and understand thy truth."

Daniel was confessing the sins of the people, and his own sins. In the Book of Judges the Bible tells us in Chapter 17 and verse 6, "In those days there was no king in Israel, for everyone did what was right in his own eyes." And the Bible said that all the ways of a man are right in his own eyes - we can always justify what we do. We can always say it is somebody else's fault, or it's the way I was raised, or it's some genetic flaw, or it's some hereditary flaw that makes me be sinful, and rebellious and destructive.

He said, "Oh Lord, righteousness belongs to you, but to us shame of face, as it is this day to the men of Judah. To the inhabitants of Jerusalem and all Israel, those near and those far off, and all the countries to which you have driven them because of the unfaithfulness they have committed against you." Our sins are committed against God. It's God that we sin against, and it is God we'll answer to.

"To you, oh Lord belongs righteousness." You say, "I don't agree with God." But God is always right. God doesn't make mistake. He's God. He is righteous, and his judgments are right and righteous. This is what Daniel is saying, "Your judgments upon this nation and upon me, they're righteous Lord." We deserve it, but now you have said that the time of judgment is over, let us be restored to mercy. In the 14th verse, he said, "Therefore the Lord has kept the disaster in mind, and brought it upon us, for the Lord our God is righteous, and all the works which He does, though we may not have obeyed his voice." Calamity came to Daniel in spite of his personal righteousness, because he was a part of a nation that was sinful. But God blessed him as an individual in the nation of Babylon, and gave him influence and power because of his righteousness. In other words, we may enter into terrible circumstances, but if we're walking with God, whatever our circumstances, God will take care of us, and see us through, and make it right. You can count on Him.

There are personal sins, and there are collective sins of the people. "Forgive us, oh Lord." Oh Lord forgive, listen, act and do not delay for your own sake my God, for your city, and for your people called by your name. He said, Oh Lord, for your own sake be honored and restore Jerusalem. Rebuild the Temple, bring the people back. And Daniel prayed, and prayed, and prayed, and it seems as though the answer wasn't going to come. Then the Angel comes to him and begins speaking to him; verses 22 - 23. "Now, while I was speaking, and praying, and confessing my sins to the people of Israel, presenting my supplication before the Lord in the holy mountain, Gabriel came." The angel Gabriel came and visited him and said in effect, "Daniel, from the first day I heard your prayer, but there were some spiritual battles that had to be won before I could come to you and answer the prayers. For the power of the prince of Persia resisted me, but now I am here and I'm going to give you understanding, and I'm going to tell you what is going to happen to the nation of Israel, and to the world in the future."

And now the next few verses follow, the most important prophecy in all of the Bible. "The time is coming, and when the walls of Jerusalem begin to be built," that means when the people have returned to Jerusalem and begun to build the walls. He said, "Seventy weeks are going to transpire." And you read it closely, it is seventy weeks of years, or four hundred and ninety years. And then he said, something incredible is going to happen, the prince is going to enter the streets of Jerusalem. And they're going to have a celebration, and we call that Palm Sunday. Now if you take the date, from the day that they begin to rebuild the walls of Jerusalem, until the day that Jesus came into Jerusalem, and the triumphant entry it was exactly seventy weeks of years, or four hundred and ninety years. God fulfilled that prophecy to the minute.

God gave Daniel understanding. Verse 24 talks about the prophecy concerning Jerusalem and the holy place in the Temple. And God stirred up Zerubbabel and then Ezra, Nehemiah, and they fulfilled their prophecy. And Jesus came into the city of Jerusalem, and the people of Israel were to embrace the Savior as Messiah, and the world would have turned to Christ as they shared the good news of God's love throughout the world. But they rejected him, and crucified him. And now the prophecy of the seventy weeks has been put in suspension, because at the end of the sixty ninth week of years, there are seven years of that four hundred and ninety years yet to be fulfilled. And that will happen during the tribulation, when God lifts His church out of the earth to be in His presence. At the end of that time He will bring His church back to the earth to rule and reign. And there will be peace and justice, and mercy, for God will rule the earth.

Daniel in prayer was given understanding of that prophecy. If you want to understand what is happening in your life, why you're going through tests and trials, or what kind of a future you have, God said "I want to give you a hope and a future." I've got a future for you. If you pray, I will reveal it to you. And how should we pray? First of all, repentance. God I'm sorry for my sins; I hate my sins, I hate what they are doing in my life, I hate what they are doing to the people that are in my life, I hate what it's doing to my nation. God deliver us as a people, as an individual. Lord, I confess I've sinned and I need forgiveness.

James 5:16 said, "Confess your faults one to another, and pray for one another, that you may be healed. The effectual fervent prayer of a righteous man availeth much." God delays giving us so many blessings, such a hope and such a future, because we first of all fail to acknowledge that we are sinners. One of the hardest things to do, is to unconditionally admit that we are wrong.

So how do we pray? We begin to worship the mighty and gracious, and powerful, and awesome God. We begin to pray "Lord;

not my will, but yours be done." Not my kingdom but your kingdom. Forgive me of my sins, cleanse my heart through the sacrifice of your son Jesus. And let me enter into fellowship with you that you might guide my steps, through the treasure trove of hope and blessings that you have waiting for me, by faith and prayer in you to unlock.

Father, in Jesus' name, forgive me of my sins, purify and cleanse my wicked heart, deliver me from the power of the evil one who seeks to rob, to steal, to destroy, to rip off the good things in my life that you have for me. For we are a sinful people, and we are a people that are wrapped up in the transitory things of life. And we're not building our hope on that which is eternal, but that which is temporal. So purify us, and cleanse us, and speak to our hearts in Jesus' name.

THE PRAYER OF HEALING

Demons and Disciples
Mark 3:7-35

This morning we're continuing our study in the Book of Mark, and we're going to be in Mark Chapter 3, starting with verses 7 and 8. When you look at the life of Jesus on earth, you recognize that though He came as a servant, He was a servant who had authority. He had the power to exercise divine authority. The first thing that Christ teaches us about His ministry on earth is that He understands and knows us. You ever feel misunderstood? I think most of us do one time or another. Sometimes you feel like nobody knows you well. The Bible says of Jesus, that He didn't need anyone to tell Him what was in a man's inner being. He simply knows what's in us. He completely understands every human being. You are understood, I am understood by God. And God loves you and loves me. And He knows what brings us to ultimate fulfillment and happiness. And usually, what God wants for us is what enriches us. Whereas what we want for ourselves usually doesn't work out too well.

"Oh Lord, if you'll just give me this man and let him marry me, I'll be happy for life. Lord if you give me this woman…'" and then, if you don't get close to God, and continue to grow in your relationship, you'll wake up one morning and look at the pillow and say, "Oh - they're still here, they're still here. How long Oh Lord, how long?" But life, and marriage, become more precious when Christ is the center, and you honor and serve Him together. It gets better every single day.

When Jesus began teaching, crowds began to follow Him. When we read this in Mark Chapter 3 verses 7 and 8, we really don't realize the magnitude of it. But it said that Jesus withdrew from His disciples to the sea, and a great multitude from Galilee followed Him, and from Judea, and Jerusalem, and Idumaea, and beyond the Jordan, and from Tyre and Sidon. And when they heard of the things He was doing, they came to Him. When you read the names of these various places, you realize that it encompasses well over a hundred miles. It goes all the way down to the Arabian Desert, all over this area, even clear up in Tyre and Sidon which is a part of modern Lebanon now. And these people were walking. That was really the only means of transportation, except for a very few rich who would have a chariot, or ride on horseback, or mules or donkeys.

It wasn't just a few people. Theologians, and people that study the times and the place and the numbers of people that were there, said that literally tens of thousands of people began to follow this prophet who healed the sick, who cast out devils, who did marvelous works. And they were astounded at His works. Can you imagine being a part of a crowd of tens of thousands, and perhaps being one of the few to press in and touch Him? And everywhere He went He was so popular.

I believe that among many things, Mark is also talking about the emptiness of popularity. There's something about us, in our culture, if you draw a crowd, you're popular. If you have a large following, you're popular. But there's emptiness in that. How many famous people have ended up pursuing relief from the emptiness in them, through using drugs and alcohol, and even suicide? I remember something Berry McGuire said to me a long time ago. He was an entertainer. He strove, and worked until he finally got to the top of the entertainment world for a while. And he said, "I got up to the penthouse and I was being 'coptered here and 'coptered there", and he said, "I strove for that, I worked for that. When I finally got to the top and I realized there was nothing there. I was so empty I didn't even want to live."

There were crowds following Jesus. It was at the peak of His popularity. But there was a reason for that; Mark is talking about the emptiness of popularity without purpose, without having the living word of God. I'm deeply concerned when I hear of many, many sermons going out that have so little scripture in them, and so much pop psychology, yet they are called Christianity. Because that won't sustain us through the realities of life, through the challenges of life. It is the living Word of God, and the personal relationship with Jesus that will sustain us. And that's the only thing that will.

So they came from miles around. But the main reason was that many people were miraculously healed of their sicknesses. You say, "What was God's purpose in healing?" Part of it was to alleviate the suffering. But the main purpose of Christ performing physical healings on earth, was to show people that He had also come to heal the spiritual sickness in us. To make us whole spiritually. Because sooner or later, we will get sick, or we'll have an accident, something violent will happen in our physical body, and our life will be separated in that violent rending called death. That will ultimately happen. But if the spirit is whole, and if the spirit is healed, and the spirit is in relationship with God, then it's just a little bump, speed bump in the road of life. And we go right into the presence of God, and begin our eternal service with our King and Lord, in the new heaven and the new earth wherein righteousness dwells. And we shall see and experience things for all eternity. The greatest of which is seeing Jesus face to face; we'll see it forever, it will never pass away.

Mark is talking about this in Mark Chapter 3 verses 9 and 10. He told the disciples that a small boat should be kept ready for Him, lest the multitudes should crush Him. For He healed so many that had afflictions, they pressed around Him to try and touch Him. Jesus said, literally, I need to have a boat to get away for there are so many people pressing in among these thousands that have needs to touch me, that they will literally crush me. Now, Jesus could have done all sorts of things; He could have put an invisible wall around Him, where people could only get so close. He could have singled out some big powerful surly bodyguards; no. He just told His disciples, there comes a time when we have to get away from the crowds, and in a very practical human manner, He said get a little boat. When we get out into the lake, they won't be able to go with us. We can have a break to carry on the other business that the Father has.

I believe that Jesus healed the body to show humanity, and show that He could also do it for the spirit. His main mission was not healing the sick, as wonderful and fulfilling as that was. His main mission was to heal the soul, to heal the spirit. I remember what my life was when I was living in rebellion against God. I had an emptiness that absolutely nothing I could do would satisfy. And I gave it my best effort. I put all of my energy and all of my drive into it, and at that age I had plenty. But the emptiness was still there. Because I knew the truth. I had an experience with God, I chose not to walk with Him for a period in my life and He let me do that, and preserved me through it.

"So get this little boat," He said. "I come, and I heal, and it draws people, but my mission is to preach and to teach." That's the mission, to teach people about God, about Jesus. In the third chapter of Mark, verse 11, the Bible said "And unclean spirits wherever they saw Him, fell down before Him and cried out saying, 'You are the Son of God'." Jesus did not choose to accept the testimony of demons, even though what they were saying was true. Satan had a plan, and a purpose in that; he wanted to identify his demonic forces with Jesus. We still see that going on. There are people that live the most wicked, morally unclean life, that wear crosses around their neck, identifying with Jesus. There are entertainers who violate all of the major commandments in the Bible. And not only violate them, but propagate them with pride, and say the most vile and the most horrible things and lead masses of young people astray. But they wear the cross. There are people living in all manner of sexual sins who say they're Christians, but do not live as the scriptures teach.

In Christ there is no grey; it's either light or dark. He's the light of the world. He illuminates. There are no shadows in Him. People would associate with demons, and they'd seek to associate them with Jesus, and Jesus would instead tell them to be quiet and cast them out. Because He didn't want their testimony. But

He delivered the people who were in bondage to these evil spirits. There are so many people that I've dealt with over the years, that don't know why they do the things that have destroyed their lives. They've destroyed their families, they've destroyed their relationships, they've destroyed their careers. They get involved in things that drag them on a downward spiral that, unless they repent, ends up in the pits of hell. What a tragedy. The scripture tells us , the Devil is a thief, he's come to steal, to kill, and destroy. But Jesus said "I've come that you might have life," and have it more abundantly. Satan wants to rob you of every good thing God has for you. He wants to take. And how does he do it? Through the lust of the flesh, the lust of the eye wanting to possess everything we see, and the pride of life. Being proud of our position, or our status, or our standing in the society, or in the culture.

They wanted to associate demons with Jesus but He put authority to cast out demons over the twelve chosen men He called. In Mark Chapter 3 verses 13 through 19, "And He goeth up into a mountain, and calleth unto Him whom He would: and they came unto Him. And He ordained twelve, that they should be with Him, and that He might send them forth to preach. And to have power to heal sicknesses, and to cast out devils: And Simon He surnamed Peter; and James the son of Zebedee, and John the brother of James; and He surnamed them Boanerges, which is, 'the sons of thunder': and Andrew, and Philip, and Bartholomew, and Matthew, and Thomas, and James the son of Alphaeus, and Thaddaeus, and Simon the Canaanite, and Judas Iscariot, which also betrayed Him: and they went into a house."

You see Jesus didn't want evil spirits, or people who were trying to exploit His popularity representing Him. He wanted people who had an experience with Him. All of these people at that time, had experienced the revelation that the Messiah was in their presence. They had a relationship with Jesus. You know it's kind of interesting; God doesn't want us to go out and to be His advocates, He doesn't want us to go out and tell people what a wonderful lifestyle Christianity is. And how neat it is, and how wonderful it is, and how if you give your life to Christ, the whole family will sing kumbaya three times a day and lie down in peace at night. That's not what Christianity is. Christianity is knowing Jesus Christ, the risen Son of God; having Him in our lives, not only as our friend but our Lord and Master. That's where it starts. That's where real ministry starts, in your relationship with Jesus. And so He called these twelve to be His witnesses, and they were the ones that were to go out and to carry on the work that He had begun.

We are witnesses to our own experience with Jesus. I've talked about it many times, but all of us have a job. We all have a message to bring to people. And what is that message? On this moment, I gave my life to Jesus Christ. I turned my heart over to Jesus. He changed my life, He transformed me. He healed my marriage, He healed my home. He did all of these wonderful things. If I was left alone and cast aside, He fulfilled me with a consciousness of how valuable I am, because He showed me how much He loved me. And how important I am to Him, and of the fact that He has a work, and a purpose for me to serve in my life. Everything that begins as a ministry begins first and foremost with a personal relationship with Jesus Christ. And that's what we should be talking about; what Jesus has done for us, and what He is doing in our lives, and what it means to us.

Now, I know this is kind of a strange place to interject this, but I know to some of my friends that I've become a little obnoxious, probably have been for a long time, but I've become aware of this recently. The Lord blessed me with this crazy little dog. That dog gets by with things in the house that I can't get by with; I've never chewed a couch up. And I end up talking about that little dog too much, you know. I love taking him walking. I walk, he swims. I walk along the lake as fast as I can walk, he goes fifty to a hundred yards off shore and he swims and he keeps up with me. That's all he does. He swims. He thinks he's a seal; he doesn't even know that he's a dog. He barks like a seal actually, when I think about it. But I have so much fun that I talk about it, and then sometimes I begin to wonder; how much do I talk about Jesus?

Oh, I'm so excited about my hobby. Once in a while I play golf; praise God, I broke a hundred and twenty. We talk about things. What happens when you fall in love with somebody; "Oh I met the most wonderful woman," or "I met the most wonderful man. Oh you just can't tell how incredible they are, they're just perfect, they don't do anything wrong, and everything is blah blah blah..." Well yeah, it'll come later, but anyway, that's kind of the way it happens. And over the years you begin to have this incredible love, and respect, for this person that walks through life with you, and you want to talk about them. The things that mattered to you the most, you talk about. Jesus said "You shall be witnesses unto me both in Jerusalem and Samaria, Judea and to the utter most parts of the earth." You shall talk about me. You are going to talk about it, how Jesus delivered me from the power of Satan, and sin, and eternal death and separation from God, and hell. This is what Mark is teaching us. This is what Jesus is speaking to us about.

Now, there is a scripture that has caused a lot of consternation in people. A lot of concerns. When Jesus was continuing His ministry, the crowds were crashing in around Him. I'm just going to tell you quickly, all of this morning is in Mark Chapter 3, verses 7 through verse 35, so I'm not going to take the time to read, I'll just tell you about the scriptures. Jesus was pressed, and He was ministering to people, and His family decided He was beside Himself, which is what is said in the scripture. So Mary and His earthly brothers, they came to talk to Him, and they said "You're going to have to...." they tried to physically remove Him from the masses, thinking that He was so consumed with His ministry they had to get Him out of there. And when they were trying to drag Him away, and they were saying "You're beside yourself," then His enemies, the Pharisees, the teachers, they said, "Aha. He is demon possessed, He's full of darkness, He's full of evil."

And so Jesus took them aside. For these people were saying He was of the Devil, that He was the prince of devils, because He cast out devils. And then Jesus said, "If a kingdom is divided against itself, it cannot stand. If Satan is divided against himself, his kingdom will not stand." He said "I am defeating Satan, I have the power to overcome Satan, I have the power to cast out demons and deliver people from that bondage." And so, He said I've not come to do anything but to destroy the work of the Devil, and to bring men back in fellowship with the Creator. That's what I'm here for. I've healed sick bodies, but every sick person that was healed eventually dies; yet their soul lives forever. All of those crowds that turned their lives over to Jesus, they'd been in Heaven for 2000 years, plus. They're still there. They said "Your mother and your brothers, they want you to get out of here to get some rest." And Jesus said something that really, was very powerful. He looked around at the circle, and those who set about Him, and He said, "Here are my mother and my brothers. For whoever does the will of God is my brother and my sister and my mother."

Now, we are to honor and to respect our families, our father and mother; the Bible teaches us that in no uncertain terms. We are to provide for those of our household; the Bible teaches that clearly in 1 Timothy 5:8. But the closest relationships we have are with believers. When you gave your life to Christ, I became your brother. You say "I don't want you." It doesn't matter, I'm in the family. You became my sister. The relationship between believers is a strong and eternal relationship. It will never change for all eternity. And it is the most important relationship we have. Our family relationships are vital, and we have to love, and respect, and to honor and cherish our family relationships, and our blood relatives. But the closest relationships you have when you become of Christ, you become a member of the body of Jesus Christ. You're literally a part of His body. And God has a ministry for you and for me. He has a place to serve, and the Holy Spirit's here to accomplish that through our lives. And the Bible tells us the way this will happen is, "When He the helper came whom I shall send to you from the Father, the Spirit of truth, who precede from the Father, He will testify of me."

And so my prayer is, Lord, pour out of your Holy Spirit upon us a body of believers, fill our hearts with such love for Jesus that we can't be quiet about it, that we have to talk about it, that we have to share it, that we have to tell people about the goodness of God and the love of God.

PRAYER FOR OUR DAILY NEEDS

Bread, Temptation, Forgiveness
Luke 11: 3-4

My father was a great man of prayer. He started praying every day at 5 a.m. Although my father knew the scripture, he had one theological error, he believed God was hard of hearing, because he prayed very loud every morning. And my brother and I would hear him. I don't know if he did it deliberately, but it came right through the vent. And I'd hear him say, "Oh Lord, and you know Louis....," and I'd put the pillow on my ears, but I couldn't get away from the power of that prayer.

He was a man of prayer. At a ministers' convention they asked him - there was a little disagreement, shocking as it is in a conference - so they asked him to pray. When he got through, a man came up and said, "Would you tell me how you can pray such powerful prayers without writing anything, and just praying?" My dad just looked at him, and said one word; "Practice." So when you pray - when you do something over and over - you get fairly proficient at it. Unless it's golf.

Let's pray. Father, thank you for the Word, we pray that you'll open our hearts to receive the truth. We ask this in Jesus' name, Amen.

We've been talking about prayer in earlier messages, going through the Book of Luke and parts of Matthew, talking about the prayers of Jesus. But here's the final part of a prayer that we are all familiar with. It is a model of prayer that takes in the whole experience of our life on earth. The Bible teaches us that we should pray for the needs of our daily lives. There are some people that say we shouldn't do that; but we should. Luke 11: 3-4 reads "Give us day by day our daily bread. And forgive us our sins; for we also forgive every one that is indebted to us. And lead us not into temptation; but deliver us from evil." This is the amazing thing about the scriptures. In these two short verses, God can bring the most profound thoughts that anyone can immediately understand.

"Give us this day our daily bread." Now, when the Bible talks about giving us our daily bread, it's not talking about just a literal loaf of bread and that's it. When He is talking about 'give us our daily bread', this is a prayer for the whole man; body, soul and spirit. It points directly to the greatest needs in our lives, and covers every aspect of our lives. All areas of our life are addressed in these two verses; so, this is a guide for our prayers to follow.

One of the first things to remember is that God is interested in everything in your life. I've heard people say, "Well, God's not interested in this little thing, I'll take care of it myself." God is interested in everything in your life. God is fully cognizant of every thought that we have, every longing, every desire, every sorrow, every joy. God is fully engaged, and has an awareness of every aspect of the life of every human being. You say, "Man, I can't grasp that." Well, I can't either, I'm not God. I'm not even God junior. I'm just a plain old human being with limited abilities, who just believes and trusts God and trusts His Word. So God wants to be involved in every aspect of our lives.

It's interesting when we go through the Bible. There were so many times Jesus would heal a number of people, such as the blind men, but only one would come back to thank Him. Most of the people that Jesus healed or delivered or made provision for, never came back to thank Him. At least there's no record of it in the scripture. There's one thing that is important in our lives; that as God answers prayers, and as God responds to our prayers, we give Him praise, we thank Him for the blessings that have come into our life. I was talking some years back to a parent who had sacrificed greatly for his children, provided for them at his own expense. He and his wife had given up many, many things in their lives, so their children could have an education. "You know I love my children," he said, "But it breaks my heart that we give them everything, and we don't do it for thanks, but," he says, "They don't ever seem to come and thank us. They just want more and more. Even if we don't have anything left to give, they're not thankful for what we have given."

Our Heavenly Father deserves our praise. I've been praying a lot these past few months, and of course for a few years, in fact many, many years. But I'm careful to give Him thanks. There's not a day that goes by that I don't thank Him for the wife he has given me, for the blessing she is in my life. For the guidance, for the wisdom, for the prayer life, for the faith. I thank Him for the daughter God gave us. I thank Him for building this place to worship. But more importantly, I thank Him for the people who have worshiped here, and are worshiping here over the years. I'm thankful for my friends. And I give God thanks for all of the blessings that He's poured into my life.

Have you've been praising God? Have you been thanking God for the blessings He has poured into your life? 1 Thessalonian 5: 18 said, "In everything give thanks, for this is the will of God in Christ Jesus concerning you." In everything give thanks. You say, "My life isn't going so good right now." Give thanks to God; He's powerful and He can take you through this trial and will bring you to a better place. Thank Him for the fact that He will not forsake you if all your friends forsake you. Give Him thanks for that. Thank him for all the answers that He brings into our life.

We want to give God thanks for the bodies that He's blessed us with. And it's proper to pray that God gives us health, that God gives us strength, that God gives us healing, that God makes provisions for our life. It's important that we learn to pray that God gives us the food that we need, gives us the necessities of life. We're not yet glorified, but God wants to bless us. Not only our spirit and soul, but He also wants to bless us in our body.

Give us this day our daily bread. The scripture doesn't say give our weekly bread, or our monthly bread, or our annual bread; it's our daily bread. God hasn't promised to give you a warehouse full of stuff; He promised to give you enough for each today. And each day He will provide. The question is, everything our body needs

God will provide; so why pray? God already knows our needs; so why pray? Yes, He does know our needs. When we pray we're not informing God. When you've confessed to God and you say something, the Lord doesn't look over at Jesus and say, "Wow; did you know that? I never thought of that before." He's all knowing. God knows what's going on in our life. So why does He want us to pray?

What happens when we fail to pray? Some really terrible changes come into our lives. When we stop thanking God for our food, when we stop thanking God for the strength that we have, when we stop thanking God for all of the things He's provided for our daily life, there's a subtle change that comes into our lives that wars against our spirit.

This change comes when we begin to believe that we are source of all the blessing that comes into our life. "I worked hard therefore I have all these things." There's some people who work harder than you or I have ever imagined, and still don't have much. "I have it because I am more intelligent than someone else. I see greater opportunities." We may not say it out loud, but the more successful we are, the more this creeps into our lives. "I have a pattern of life that is built for success." It's built for success if God blesses you. It comes from God. We begin to take credit for everything in our lives, we believe that we are source of our own blessings, when we stop giving thanks to God for the things that He has blessed us with, and the things that He has provided for us.

We reach the point where we believe we can supply all of our own needs. You go back and look at the Book of Kings, and you read about, "This king did this, and this king did that, and they accomplish this, and did whatever was good or did evil," and whatever. But all of those verses when it talked about those kings; it always ends with the words, "and he died." And he died.

When we're not giving thanks to God we get restless, we get a little bit depressed. Dr. Harry A. Ironside was one of the great theologians, who's written many commentaries and many wonderful books. When he was a young man he went into a cafeteria to get some food. And when he got in there and looked around, every table was filled except one. There was one guy sitting over there. So he went over and said, "Sir, do you mind if I just sit here with you." He didn't know what the guy said, he kind of grunted, kind of a surly guy. So he sat down and quietly did what he always did; bowed his head, and put his hand to his brow, and he thanked God for his food. The guy looked up at him and said, "What's the matter with you? You got a headache? Are you really sad, or something, you sit head bowed?" He was mocking him. He knew what he was doing. "I don't believe in giving thanks for anything." And Ironside said, "Well, I was giving thanks for my food." The guy said again, "I don't believe in giving thanks for anything." And Ironside said to him, "Oh, you're just like my dog, he never gives thanks for anything, he just starts right in." I don't know how good a witness that was, but that's the way it is. Why? Because it speaks of our animal nature. That's the way we are. At first we get a privilege, and pretty soon we think it's a right.

God does something special, and we think if He doesn't do the same thing for us the next time, He has failed us. You look at King Nebuchadnezzar. He was one of the most powerful men on earth at that time. And he went to his great palace, with his massive walls that were so high and so wide they had chariots races around the top of them. His gardens were one of the Seven Wonders of the World. And he was walking around an evening and said, "Is not this great Babylon that I have built for royal dwelling by my mighty power for the honor of my majesty? I did all of this." And God smote his mind, and he received the mind of a beast, so much so that he couldn't be kept indoors. And for years he went out and ate grass and lived off the field just like an animal. He had long finger nails, and long hair draping all over him, and finally when he came to his senses, he had a different perspective. He recognized that God was the source of everything that he had.

There is something that happens to us if we don't give God thanks for different things — don't thank Him for our food, don't thank Him for our clothing, don't thank Him for the blessings and the people we have in our life. Suddenly we become more like the animals, in that we want something for ourselves, we feel like we have rights because we've earned it. We haven't. You could take all of your gifts, and all of your talents, and all of everything that we have, and you could go to some other country like Sudan, and see how your life would turn out. In this country we're living off the historic blessing that God has poured out upon this nation because of our past as a Godly people.

The second part of His prayer is human relationships. Luke 11:4, "Forgive us our sins as we forgive everyone who is indebted to us, or who has sinned against us." You say, "Now wait a minute, what is God saying?" God is telling you to forgive people that have wronged you, and hurt you, people that have done spite to you. You say "Why? They don't deserve it." Well did you deserve the forgiveness that God gave you? "Forgive us our trespasses as we forgive those who trespassed against us."

We need a cleansed conscience. The Bible said, "As far as it depends on you, live in peace with all men." Don't worry about what anybody else says or does. I talk about this a lot, but I'm shocked and amazed when I talk and counsel with people how many people have someone in their life they cannot forgive. And I've asked them, and they say to me, "I just simply can't forgive them." And I look at them and say, "I look at it differently; I think you simply *won't* forgive them."

You've been forgiven. Forgive us our sins and give the grace and the power to follow your example, Lord Jesus, for we sinned against you. We were a part of the human family that sent you to the cross to die and give us access to God. Lord, forgive us our sins. You see something is going to change in our life. Even psychologists and some doctors recognize that when we have unresolved conflict towards others in our life, it can affect our health. We can have palpitations of the heart, anxiety, and sleeplessness. We can have a troubled mind and a disturbed life. And some of it goes right to the fact there are people who have wronged us or harmed us. At least we believe that's the case, and we have not forgiven them.

We keep reminding people of what we've done. There's husbands and wives who have been unfaithful to each other, and we say "We forgive," and we say "We're reconciled." But until God works a miracle in our heart, and in the hearts of the others involved in these things, we never truly forgive. And they never truly enter into that place of trust, and rest, and peace. There's always anxiety. Yes, it's a terrible wrong. Yes, there are people that have cheated us in business and lied to us. Yes, there are people who have abused us, have spoken against us, in all sorts of vile manners that weren't even true. But the Bible said "Forgive us our sins as we forgive others of their sins against us," and when you do that you are suddenly free.

One of the things that I practice in prayer, and have throughout my ministry, I ask God to search my heart. "Lord, if I have any bitterness, any anger, any resentment of anyone, forgive me. And Lord, I will do anything I can to reconcile with that person." When you truly do that, there's a peace that comes over your life. You say, "Well, what if they don't respond?" They probably won't. I'm going to tell you that in advance. If you go and ask their forgiveness they probably - unless God does a work in their heart - they will just give you another battle to overcome. But nonetheless, you can walk away free from that. They have no power over you any longer when you finally give that up to God.

We have a need for a clean conscience. We really do. We really have a need to have that clouded conscience cleared up, and have peace with God. There are two things that really affect our emotional health, and sometimes it even creeps over into our physical health; fear, and guilt. If we're guilty about something we've done toward somebody, or we have fear about things, these things can affect our physical body. "Forgive us our sins." God promised us in Romans Chapter 8 verse 1, "There is therefore now no condemnation for those who are in Christ Jesus who do not walk according to the flesh, but according to the Spirit."

You see, our forgiveness is precious, because God forgives us our sins based on the death of Jesus Christ, His sinless son on the cross. That's the basis; that's how we come to God. Ephesian 1:7 said, "In Him we have redemption through His blood, the forgiveness of His sins according to the riches of His grace." Grace means unmerited favor. We've done nothing to earn it, He just forgives us and loves us by His grace. Well you say, "I can't forgive these folks. I can't forgive this." I'm saying by the grace of God, by the power of the Spirit, you can forgive. And the only thing that will keep you from forgiving is that you refuse to turn it loose. You won't forgive. But you will remain in bondage to that person, or that circumstance, until you do. And it will affect your health, it will affect your happiness and peace, and contentment in your life. God wants to heal that.

The Bible said in Matthew 5:24, that even in giving ourselves, and our time and our resources to God, we need to be reconciled to brothers and sisters we are in conflict with. Scripture said, "Leave there thy gift before the altar, and go thy way; first be reconciled to thy brother, and then come and offer thy gift." First make things right with your brother and then come and offer your gift. If we receive forgiveness we must extend forgiveness. This is a part of God teaching us to pray.

How am I going to forgive? You pray, you be honest with God. You say, "Lord I can't forgive that person they're such slime doggies.... they're not even worthy of forgiveness." And the Lord said you need to pray a little more, you know, get the slime doggie out of there. You can actually pray for that person with a clear heart and say, "Lord bless them, forgive me for hanging on to this wrong, this slight Lord, and I'm wrong by the way I responded. Lord help me." God will finally do it. He'll do it.

I've shared this with you before. Very early in my ministry, the second revival meeting that no one was revived in that I preached. And it was down in the far South, Texas, and I was thrilled to have a chance to preach. I wanted to preach so badly, and I did - but anyway I had a desire to preach so badly that I would go anywhere. Matter of fact, the first year of my evangelistic ministry I had a Morris Minor, it's a car about the same size as I am. And we'd take turns; I'd ride in it, and I'd carry it for a while. It was a sorry little car. But I drove that thing 89,000 miles, because anybody who would have me, I'd go. And here's my second meeting, and I'm so excited, and I had these great sermons, they lasted for forty-five minutes, maybe an hour. But there was a lot of sweat and energy poured into those sermons, and a lot of prayer. And the pastor came, and I thought boy, "Is he ever going to compliment me" because he said come on into my study, I want to share something with you, Louis. Okay, I was excited. He said, "Louis there's just something about you that I don't like. I can't stand you." I'd really loved the guy until then, and then I didn't like him either. You know, that's what happens.

Like I've said many times, my dad gave me some advice. He said, "Son, I'm human enough to want everybody to like me, but I'm smart enough to know they're all not gonna like me. Forgive him son." That was it. And I did forgive him. And I asked his forgiveness for whatever. Probably my sermons offended him, I don't know. I'm sure glad there were no tape recorders back then. So anyway, finally I did forgive him. And then he fired me, and I didn't get to finish the meeting.

Prayer will keep us out of temptation. "Lead us not into temptation." We might misunderstand the scripture and say, "Oh, God tempts us?" No, God never tempts us to do evil. It says, lead us not into temptation, and I believe it means "Lord, keep me from unrecognized temptations." Sometimes I'm wrong about something; I really believe I'm right, and I go ahead and push it and do it. I know I'm dead wrong about it. I now realize it was an unrecognized temptation, and I have to ask God's forgiveness and ask the forgiveness of anyone I've hurt through it. Lord keep me out of the power of the tempter, deliver me. Lord deliver me from evil. God will do these things.

You remember Peter, he said "Lord," - you will find this in Matthew 26:33, "Lord, most of these disciples here are going to forsake you. But Lord, you know me, I will not forsake you." I am the big fisherman. He was a boisterous guy. And he said to Him, "Even if all are made to stumble because of you, I will never be made to stumble." And you know the rest of the story, Jesus said, "Before the rooster crows, you would have denied me three times." You say, "Why did that happen?" You see, the Lord tried to keep him from some unintended temptation, some unintended trial. You go back to Mathew 25:41, Jesus said to Peter "Watch and pray." He knew what was coming. But Peter didn't watch and pray. He went out, laid down, closed his eyes and slept. I don't have any reasons to prove it, but I really believe if had he spent that time watching and praying, he would not have fallen. He let evil grab him. He should have been praying, but he was sleeping.

There comes a time in our lives when we must lay everything aside and say "God I need you now, I'm praying. There's nothing more important to me in my day, in my life than hearing from you. And I'm going to focus my prayer, and if you lay on my heart my past sins, I'll ask forgiveness. I'm going to pray Lord, not to inform you of anything, but to bring myself to a recognition of all I have that is good, all that is blessed. All the provisions of my life, every opportunity that I have, every blessing that I have, Lord it comes from you. It does not come from me."

And that's what prayer is for. It's not for God, it's for us. God already knows, and He already has an answer. But those answers many times are withheld until we pray.

"You have not because you ask not." That's what the scripture says.

PERSISTENT PRAYER

Knock and Ask

Matthew 7:7

You can read the Bible, and go through the same passage of scripture hundreds of times over the years, preach a number of sermons, and you suddenly realize you preached something wrong. You just didn't understand it. Then God gives you a new insight. Now that's a terrible thing for a preacher to admit, but it's just the fact. Suddenly the Holy Spirit speaks to you and says, "That's fine what you did; but there's more to it than that." So the Lord says, "Open your eyes, open your heart." And you go a little deeper, and you begin to discover the wonderful messages that come up when the Holy Spirit thinks it's time. It just grabs you.

This is an area of scripture I've addressed on numerous occasions during the course of my ministry. It's in the 11th chapter of the Book of Luke. As Jesus and the disciples were leaving the room, one of the disciples – who'd been praying – said to them, "Lord, teach us to pray." So this morning, I want to talk specifically about the power of persistent prayer. Let's pray together that the Lord will open our hearts and our understanding to receiving His Word this morning.

Father we thank you for the truth of the scripture, and we pray that you will open our hearts to receive and to perceive what you're saying to us today, that our faith and our prayer might increase in effectiveness and power as we learn to pray according to your purpose, and according to the pattern you've established for us in the scripture. And then may faith grow in our hearts, that we might reach out and embrace and receive the answer to prayers. We ask this in Jesus' name, Amen.

In addressing the subject of prayer, Jesus gives several answers. The one we'll look at begins with verse 5 of Luke Chapter 11, and runs through verse 13. We're going to take it slowly, and in sequence, and we'll start with 11:1 where it says, "Now it came to pass as He was praying in a certain place, and He sees that one of His disciples said to Him 'Lord teach us to pray as John taught his disciples.'" There are many times in the life of Jesus when people were asking Him questions, and as you go through the Bible most of the questions were asked by nonbelievers, people who were trying to trip Him up, or to give Him a challenging question that they believed He couldn't answer. One of the most familiar ones is when they asked Him "Should we pay tax to Caesar?" Of course, Caesar was the human government, and it would have been a criminal offence to say that you are not to pay taxes, kind of like America. So, He was going through that process and Jesus said, "Hand me a coin" and somebody handed Him a denarius, and he looked at it and said, "Whose image is on this?" And they said, "Caesar's." He said "Render to Caesar what is Caesar's, and to God what is God's." Now, I could have never thought of that answer. You know when you can't think of anything to say, you just talk, and talk, and talk, and hope that people would forget what they asked by the time you get through talking. You just kind of filibuster.

There are other questions though that were extremely sincere, they came from the heart. The scripture talks about some of these. There was a young ruler talked about in Chapter 18 of the Book of Luke; "And he came to Heaven and he said to Him, Lord, good teacher, what shall I do to inherit eternal life?" Now, that wasn't a trick question, that was a question that came out of a searching heart. Jesus looked at him and He knew what god that young man served. And He answered, and He said to him, "Sell everything you have, give it to the poor, and come and follow me." Here is one of the most amazing invitations in scripture, this young man could have been, perhaps, one of the disciples. "Come and follow me." But the man went away sad, because he had great possessions, his god was his money, and he was not willing to sacrifice his money for his soul. This was just an honest, sincere question that came to Jesus.

And so we go and we look into scripture. The thief on the cross was hanging there, Jesus was in the center, one thief on either side. And one of them recognized that in spite of all of the mocking, and all the harsh things being said to Jesus, there was something different about Him. And he suddenly recognized this is not only a man, but also God. And he looked over, and the simple question he said, "Lord, remember me when you come into your kingdom." And Jesus said, "Today, you shall be with me in paradise."

There's all kinds of questions asked in the Bible, and the question we're dealing with today is, "Lord, how can we pray more effectively? Teach us to pray." In verses 5 through 7 of Luke Chapter 11, He said to them, "Which of you have a friend who goes to him at midnight and says, 'Friend, lend me three loaves. I have a friend that is coming to visit me, and I don't have anything to give him. I don't have any food in the house.'" And the friend answered him, saying, effectively, "What are you doing calling me at this time at night? You want bread? I'm in bed now; not only that, but my kids are in bed, so if I get up and get you a loaf all the kids are going to wake up, and they're going to cause a big fuss, and there's not going to be any peace or rest at all tonight." And yet the friend kept asking him, and kept knocking until finally, because he persisted, his friend got out of bed and gave him some bread.

Persistence. Though he would not rise and give him because he is a friend, yet because of persistence, he will rise and give him what he needs. I've always thought that this meant that we should just keep praying, and praying, and praying for the same thing, and never give up. And yet when you read the rest of this area of scripture, that's not what it's saying at all. It's exactly the opposite. Because the next verse tells us, He says, "So I say to you 'Ask and it shall be given, seek and you shall find, knock and it shall be opened unto you, for everyone who asks receives and he who seeks finds and to him who knocks, the door is opened." And so God is saying exactly the opposite of this friend; He said you just ask and you'll receive.

Now, there's three levels of prayer that are dealt with in this area of scripture; 'ask', 'seek' and 'find.' And of course, kind of interesting that it comes up with a nice little way to remember them; "a" is the first letter of ask, "s" is the first letter of seek and "k" is the first letter of knock. So ask seek and knock, are the three levels of prayer Jesus is talking about in this particular area of scripture.

You see, we don't have to beg God, we don't have to plead with God. The scripture teaches us that He wants to bless us. He wants to minister to us. He wants to meet our needs. He is a loving God, He is a good, and a kind, and a gracious God. God is never reluctant to answer prayer. Never. He's not like that friend who doesn't want to get out of bed. Of course, God doesn't have a bed in His house anyway because He doesn't need one, and you won't have one in heaven either because you won't want to waste any of eternity sleeping.

We find that Jesus says, if a son asks bread from a father, will the father trick him, and say "Here son," and he has a rock that looks like a piece of bread and he says, "Hey, chomp down on that buddy." He said no, a father wouldn't do that. Or if he asks for a fish, would you slip him a snake, or a serpent? Or if he asks for an egg, would you give him a scorpion? He said, if you, despite being human or evil, know how to give gifts to your children, how much more shall your Heavenly Father give to those who ask Him?

From this it follows that we're giving God a bad rap by saying that He won't get up and pay attention to us, and answer our prayers. He does answer prayer; the problem doesn't lie in answering prayer, we don't perceive the answer that God is giving. He always answers; that's what the scripture teaches us, and it is absolutely true.

These three levels of prayer; the circumstances are always different, but the answer is the same. God always answers prayer. The question is, do we receive the answer? The scripture asks; is God a liar? Does God ever lie? No. God said, "I will answer you," and He doesn't lie. You can count on that. Does He say He will give, and then not give? No, that's not God. And you go on, and you think about it; is He cruel like an earthly father who wants to give you a rock instead of bread? No, He's not that way. God always gives an answer.

I told you many times, my father was not quite as godly as God, though he was a man of God, and he tricked me sometimes. When I was about seven years old, we were out rabbit hunting out in the field, and suddenly I saw my dad throwing these little things that looked like little candy drops. And I said, "Dad what is that?" He said, "Son, these are smart pills". And I said, "Can I have one?" And he said, "Sure son". And I bit it, and spat it out, and gagged. Actually it wasn't a smart pill. I said, "That was terrible!" It was actually kind of something that a rabbit had processed, and I spat it out on the ground and I said, "Dad, that was awful, why did you do that to me?" And he said, "Well son, you're smarter now, aren't you?" And I said "Yes, I guess I am". And so I'm just going to let it go with that. But our Heavenly Father doesn't trick us, He doesn't give you smart pills when you're asking Him for bread. He just simply doesn't do it. The question is not did He give, but did we receive?

In the Book of James, James is talking about our Father in verses 6 through 8 of the first chapter. He said, "But let him ask in faith, nothing wavering. For he that wavereth is like a wave of the sea driven with the wind and tossed. For let not that man think that he will receive anything from the Lord. A double minded man is unstable in all of his ways." All the gifts and graces of God come through the promises that He gives through faith.

Faith; there's an old song I think Stewart Hamlin wrote many, many years ago; *Prayer Is The Key To Heaven But Faith Unlocks The Door*. Faith is believing in God. God says what He means and means what He says, and all the gifts were given on the basis of faith, not unbelief. I can't find anything in the Bible that you'd want, that is promised to unbelief. The question is, what are we praying for? Faith takes the answer for granted. God is faithful, God gives. When I pray, when you pray, He answers. Lord give us the perception and the spirit that we might receive and understand the answers that are given.

God is faithful, whatever we need in our lives, it's there in God. He doesn't say, "I will provide you with all that you want," but "I will provide all that you need." I found myself on occasion in my life praying more for wants than for needs, and I have a little difficulty with those who say you can just speak the word of faith and get anything you want. Everything I need, all of these gifts are given on the basis of faith not unbelief; but what are we praying for?

The thing is, we have to seek. 'Seek' is another level of prayer; seeking takes time. For a while I got kind of addicted to a program about where they go out and hunt for criminals that have gotten away with crime, murder primarily, for years and years. And they go and they study the cold cases, I'm not talking about T.V. drama, I'm talking about an intellectual pursuit of real cases. I was watching the program, and I was amazed at the persistence of some of these detectives, who for years would not give up. Because they believed that someone who takes another person's life must receive punishment. And so they would go on. There was one case in particular that touched me, where a young girl had been brutally murdered, and this man stayed with it for nine years. He continued to seek for the answer; who committed this crime? So there is asking, and that is something that God responds to instantly; then there is seeking.

Seeking injects an element of time. Sometimes when we pray, we ask God for something that requires time. The answer is there, the answer is on the way, but it takes time. Seeking. I have a glorious example of seeking, that happens too often in my life, and it happened yesterday. My old grill gave up the ghost, and I finally got another one. I was so thrilled about the price I got on it, sixty percent off. I don't know if it is any good or not, but it was cheap, and I thank God for that. So I'm looking for the butane bottle, and I searched the garage. I spent almost thirty minutes going through the same places, over and over. It's a large gas bottle, and tall, and it's really hard to hide. But I couldn't find it. So I came in, and I declared to Mary, "Mary, someone stole my butane bottle. I don't know who it was." And she says, "Why would they steal that when there is so much other good stuff in there?" And I said, "Well, they probably know where to sell it." I had this whole crime scene worked out and everything. So, I get a little nervous, and I made another pass through the garage just to make sure. After that I'm convinced it's been stolen. Then Mary comes to me about five o'clock yesterday afternoon and says "I found your butane bottle." And it really ticked me off because I'd been seeking, she hadn't. She says, "It was right by your bicycle" which reminded me that I hadn't ridden that bicycle for many, many years. It's an interesting thing, and that's kind of the way it is in our home and probably a lot of homes; many times the wife is the one who knows where it is, after we've searched and searched.

So seeking God injects an element of time. There's something that I've been praying for, for decades. The answer has not come to full fruition, but I know that the answer is on the way because I'm continuing to seek in the will of God for that answer, and I'm trusting Him. And I'm believing. And regardless of how it looks on the outside, I know because of His promises, it shall come to pass. It is not 'if', it is simply 'when', because God is faithful. And that's something we need to remember. Sometimes there's an instant answer; and sometimes God is working things out.

You remember the prophet was praying and he said, "Okay, why didn't you answer me sooner?" He said, "I answered you from the first day, but the power of the Prince of Persia resisted me." There were demonic forces that God subdued before the answer came. You keep praying. You don't give up, you don't give up.

There was friend of mine that had a pit bull terrier, and he would love to take this dog and get a rope, and the dog would grip it with his jaws, and he could pick that dog up and he swing him around and around... and that pit bull would never let go. Finally it would get down, after swinging so much that he would be dizzy, and kind of wander around the yard. But it was so cool, even when he couldn't really get his bearings, because he still hung on to the rope. Lord, make us pit bulls, in prayer. Let us hang on to the word of God until the answers are coming when we seek.

Paul said three times, "I prayed that God would remove this physical ailment that I had; I had thorns in my body. Three times I asked." He had to seek, he had to wait, and finally God said "Paul, I had heard you. I know that you have this malady, I know that you have this suffering." But He said to him, "My grace is sufficient for you, for my strength is made perfect in weakness." Therefore most gladly, Paul said, "I would rather boast of my infirmities that the power of Christ might rest upon me." Prayer broke through, and he still had the physical problem. God said "I'll use it for my glory, and my grace will be sufficient to help you through this trial." Don't give up; I'm there, I heard you, I know that you're seeking me and I know that this is going to answer. Paul hungered and thirsted for righteousness, he hungered and thirsted for that desire to meet God, and to find God, and to receive God's direction.

The scripture said, "Blessed are those who hunger and thirst for righteousness." You'll find that in the Book of Mathew Chapter 5. In the Book of Romans it tells us Paul was invited to go and minister to some people, and he said he wanted to go, and he asked God if he could. But he could not go until God said so.

What Paul meant was, I want to come, but when I do, I want to come in the will of God. Because if I go out of the will of God I can't do you a bit of good. Because I'm on my own. When I'm in the will of God, God says I'm going to take care of you, I'm going to fulfill the promise. We have to make those decisions in life. What does God want me to do? Not what do I want to do.

The scripture says that we ask, and we seek, and then we knock. Knocking; if you really want to get in somewhere, you have to keep knocking until somehow the door is opened. You hang on, you know it's the will of God. You know it's what God desires, and yet you also know that there are spiritual forces that are in opposition. And so if you trust God, you know that as you knock, those forces are being subdued. Lives are being changed, prepared to receive what God has for them, and you just keep knocking. You might have a rebellious kid or young person that turned away from the Lord, is all caught up in the world. I'm going to tell you something; you keep knocking and someday they will be back. Most of them won't look like much when they get here, but they're going to come back, you can count on that. Sin is hard on us, sin takes a terrible toll on our lives. Sin adds baggage that we have to carry around. Some of it for the rest of our lives.

I remember going to the airport in Atlanta, and I decided I needed a little walk. The Atlanta airport is one of the greatest, most terrible mazes that ever existed on the earth. There are miles, literally miles of underground walkways. So I said I'm not going to take the train, I'm going to walk to the next concourse where I'm supposed to change planes. And so I walked, and I walked, and I walked. I had an hour between flights. I didn't get there until it was ten until the flight. It took me fifty minutes of walking, counting the time that I got lost. And then I finally got there. You say, "Why did you keep going?" Because I didn't want to miss my plane. I wanted to go home.

The disciples were not powerful witnesses until the resurrection of Jesus, when He fulfilled the prophecy of David. David prophesized, and he said, "He shall receive gifts for men." And the scripture said in Acts, "He gave gifts to men." David said when the Messiah came, He would die, rise again and pour out gifts upon men. And He told his disciples "Don't even begin to try to witness until the Holy Spirit comes upon you." And He said what you have to do is… you have to what? He said, wait, wait upon God. Knock, knock, knock until the Spirit comes and empowers you. And it transformed their lives from being frightened, fearful witnesses, to being powerful witnesses, as the Holy Spirit of God came and became their helpers.

Persistence in prayer brings victory. Faith comes through persistence in prayer. We might be weak in prayer, but the more we pray, the greater our faith. The more we meditate upon God, the more we receive from God. The more we look into the Book, and see the promises, and lay claim to them, the more we receive from God. You want to know; it's an interesting thing, the disciples on the day of Pentecost were baptized in the spirit, but we find numerous occasions in the Bible when they needed to be recharged. And they would pray again and be renewed in the Holy Spirit. You find out in the scripture that it is not a one-time experience. It is a constant renewal of the Spirit in our lives. Sometimes we get weak and faint, we get weary physically, we get burned out, we get kind of beat up and battered… and it's time to go back and say, "Lord renew me in your Spirit."

After the loving kindness of our God appeared, He ministered to us and He poured out upon us the renewing of the Holy Spirit which He poured out abundantly upon our lives. He said, "You shall receive the power of God through the work of the Holy Spirit and you shall be witnesses to me in Jerusalem, Samaria and to the uttermost parts of the earth." And this Bible is true; you don't have to beg God and say, "God, get out of bed."

PRAY OR LOSE HEART

When There's No Place to Turn
Luke 18:1-8

This morning we have titled the message, "Pray or Lose Heart". Or, as it's termed in the King James Version, "Pray or Faint". Sometimes we wonder why God wants us to pray. He already knows what is best for us, He already knows that He wants to give us these things, and yet sometimes we don't pray correctly. We pray for things that are not His will, not His purpose. Prayer doesn't change God. He is the unchangeable God, the scripture says. Prayer changes us. Prayer doesn't move God into conformity to our will, prayer moves us into conformity with God's will. It makes us effective instruments for God to use for His glory, for His kingdom.

Lord, we thank you for the access you've given us to yourself. It is such a privilege to come into your magnificent and eternal, all-seeing and all-knowing presence. To not only have fellowship with you but, through your son Jesus, to be your friend. And Lord, we want to prepare our minds, our spirits, bodies, souls, all of us to be sufficiently in tune with you that we will know your voice and recognize your directions, your instructions, your encouragement, whatever we need you to pour into our lives. And when we ask, we want to ask not according to our will, but according to yours.

You said we can ask whatever we wish if we're asking in a way that the Father will be glorified in the Son. And we thank you for your Word that guides us into prayer communion with you. We look at your greatness, your majesty, and your power, and we compare that to our problems, and they diminish. In ourselves they seem overwhelming. But when we measure our challenges in relationship to the greatness of God, they fade into insignificance, leaving us with peace. Speak to our hearts through the Word today Father, and give us spiritual understanding of what the Spirit would say to the church today. We ask this in the name of our Lord and our Savior, our Friend, our Deliverer Jesus Christ, Amen.

In the Book of Luke Chapter 18, verses 1 through 8, Jesus shows us how to pray. He spoke a parable that illustrated how men ought always to pray and not to lose heart. In the King James Bible it says and "not faint". Lose heart or faint. Those are two expressions that in the biblical sense mean the same thing.

Jesus' parable spoke of a certain city in which there was a judge who neither feared God nor had regard for men. Now, there was a widow in that city, and she came to him saying, "Get justice for me from my adversary." At first he would not do so, but afterward he said within himself; "Though I do not fear God nor regard men, yet because this widow troubles me, I will avenge her lest by her continued coming she wearies me. I'm afraid she will tire me. She just won't quit, she keeps coming."

Then the Lord said, "Hear what the judge said, and shall God not avenge His own elect who cry out day and night to Him though He bears long with them? I tell you, He will avenge them speedily; nevertheless when the Son of Man comes will He really find faith on the earth?" Now, these words on prayer fall from the lips of Jesus immediately after the preceding verses which were talking about the Second Coming of Christ. And when you look at this there is a correlation between watchfulness and prayer.

I can remember years ago we were flying on our way to India, stopping briefly in Africa. And our daughter was at that time just a baby, a little girl of two or three years old. She loved it when there was turbulence because she had been on airplanes most of her life. We travelled all the time, ministering in different parts of the world. We had this terrible storm and the plane was flying up in the air and it would suddenly fall, and it would boom, and you would look out and see the wings flap. That was the first time I realized the wings had a little give in them, they looked like a pelican trying to take off. And pillows were flying and stuff was flying around in the airplane. One of the stewardess was crying. That's not a good sign. I noticed that in that plane there were many different religions, and everybody seemed to be praying. Except my daughter; she was going, "Whoopee, let's do it again." She didn't recognize the potential peril that we were in.

Prayer; there is a correlation that comes between a crisis and an emergency and prayer. There is a correlation between watchfulness and prayer. When we look at what's happening in our nation, thousands and thousands of babies destroyed before they take their first breath. We look at the crime, we look at the tragedy of young people whose lives are wrecked before they reach their 20th birthday. They're in bondage to all sorts of vices that war against them having any joy or fulfillment in life. Look at the government that is so confused, with little ability to see the facts and accept them, or unite the nation to do something about the problems.

This nation grew and prospered because, in spite of all our sins and failings, we were a nation that looked first to God. It's on our coins. When I was in school we opened the school day with prayer over the loud speaker. We would also have a little devotional that the students would give. We talked about God. That wasn't unusual, it was common in most schools throughout the United States. There was a reliance on God, and when war would come or crisis would come prayer would come too. Then we thought there would never be a time when the nation would turn to prayer again, but then came 9/11, and we became a praying nation once more.

We quickly forget how God answered our prayers and how God protected us down through these years. We passed through these crises and tended to forget the one who stilled the troubled waters and brought peace to our hearts, who protected us from enemies. But the scripture says Jesus spoke in parables; He said, we ought always to pray, not lose heart, and not faint. And there is a correlation here; if you don't pray you will lose heart. Sooner or later, something will come in your life, something that will devastate you. Not just when you're older, it can come at any stage; if you don't pray you will lose heart. There will be circumstances in life that will surround you, until you feel there is no way out, and no hope, and you look at the problem and see the hopelessness of your circumstances and you begin to lose faith. And you lose heart.

The only cure for it is prayer. Because when you pray, you are talking to the one who can solve any problem, who can change any life, who can turn any circumstance around, who can provide for any need. A God who truly loves and cares about you. This is why we should pray. This is why it's so important.

Now, these words on prayer come from the lips of Jesus, and we have this correlation, this contrast of principles; on the one side a just and loving God, on the other side an unjust judge who doesn't fear God and doesn't fear men. And opposed to the judge is a widow seeking justice. She has no money, no political influence, no family influence, no voting block to get him out of office, no way to have justice brought to her. But she uses the one thing that she does have available; she keeps coming back. And she keeps coming back, and she keeps coming back, until finally he gives in. Not because he is just, but simply because she wore him out.

You ever had a child that wanted something? And you say "No," and they think of 487 reasons, and they bring them all. One at a time they slip them in, just one after another. They know how. My four-year-old daughter was riding with her grandparents. Her granddad didn't care much about keeping his car polished, so there was plenty of dust on the dashboard. And she drew a big circle on the dashboard, and she said to her granddad; "Grandpa, I want to show you something about my parents. When I want something, this circle is here. If I go to my dad, I go right through that circle and I get it. But when I go to my mom, I move here and I hit a little hard spot, so I'll have to back up and find another way. I will hit another hard spot, then another hard spot." And she smiled and said, "But Grandpa, I always find a way to get past those hard spots."

Well, God doesn't have any hard spots. He is not trying to withhold anything from you. The Bible said, "He will not withhold any," what? "Any good thing from you. I will not withhold anything that is for your benefit," for your growth. God doesn't have those hard spots. He wants you to commune with Him and to find out the blessings that He has in store for you so that you don't lose heart. So that you don't give up. There is His contrast of principles. We ought always to pray and not lose heart. So our choice is, and I say it again, we either pray or ultimately we will lose heart. It will happen.

People without faith sometimes seem to have exciting and fulfilling lives. They don't have God, but life seems to be just a big bowl of cherries. I used to enjoy some of Ernest Hemmingway's stories when I was a young guy. He always seemed like the ultimate adventurer, the man that went out and lived life to the fullest and squeezed the last drop out of the orange. He just had this incredible life. But then you look at how he ended up. Empty, disillusioned, no faith in God, no hope for the future. He sat in a cabin and put a shotgun to his mouth and pulled the trigger with his toes.

I think about the young man from Seattle, Cobain. Millions of kids admired him, his concerts were packed out, money was pouring in. He had a platform, he had influence... and he also found a shotgun.

We lost another great talent, just a young scared kid in my belief. Whitney Houston, she knew the words, she knew the gospel, but she couldn't live it. Her life was burned out, the gift of music and voice that God gave her had already been destroyed by drugs.

If we don't have contact with God, we will burn out, and we will lose hope, and we will faint, and we'll come to a place in our life where there is nothing there to sustain us. The problem that we face in this culture is that we have a new religion. Oh yes, we still have Christianity and the Bible. We do a little marriage, we do funerals and that kind of thing. But in our daily lives for most Americans, God is not a priority.

We have science. We have the false teaching of evolution that seeks to explain our origins, and does it so unsuccessfully. It speaks of a cold impersonal universe that has set laws that march on, and man is like a little ant that crawls around on the sphere - not even as big as an ant in the scope of the universe. We're only here for a short time. Jesus said, "We're like grass that comes today and tomorrow it's thrown into the fire." It doesn't last very long.

When we believe in evolution, there's no governing power in the universe and we have no particular meaning. We're just an accident of nature, a creation made to live for a period of time and then die. And with that false teaching of evolution we bow down to the God of science. The theory of evolution won't comfort us, or guide us, or direct us. Science can't fill the emptiness within our soul that only God can fill.

Science is a God that has no father. But we have a heavenly Father that we contact with prayer, and He wraps His arms of love around us. He stills our fear, He gives us hope and He causes us not to faint but to grow stronger, because we recognize the greatness of His power, and compassion, and love. And that with Him, all things are possible. There is nothing that is hopeless in God. There is no circumstance, there is no challenge that any of us face that is beyond the power of our loving Father.

He is a Father who cares and a Father who understands, a Father who unlike our earthly fathers, always has time to listen, who has limitless power to help us. The Psalmers wrote in Psalm 103:13, "As a father pities his children so the Lord pities those who fear him." He has a father's love and a father's strength that reaches out to us, and the only thing that withholds His blessing and His peace from our lives is our absence in the place of prayer.

Someone told me the other day, they simply don't have time to pray. Ten minutes later they were giving me a detailed account of the last five football games. "I don't have time." I will tell you something folks, life will create circumstances where football won't do it for you. Our diversions won't help, television won't solve the problem, movies won't solve the problem. Our fun and games and all the things that we pursue won't mean a thing. And the wonderful thing is that the scripture says we have a "Father who upbraideth not", that's a father who doesn't scold us.

When you've really messed up and your father says, "I told you this was going to happen, you know, don't do this." And then finally it happened, and it's so bad, and you have to go back and say, "Dad you were right." And the father goes into his wonderful litany. "If you'd listened to me, you wouldn't be in this mess. When I was growing up I didn't make any mistakes. I just had a lot more strength than you do and I was a lot better person. So if you would listen to me in the future..." Well that kid is not going to listen to you. He's going to say, "Well I would rather die than confess."'

That's not the kind of Father we have. God doesn't recite our past to us. He already knows it, and so do we. He just forgives. And when we begin to pray and we get contact with Him, we have this conversation with God. It's hard to have a relationship without communication! You know what's happened, we've all experienced it in life; we get into some kind of conflict with somebody that we love, our wife or child or friend, and they say to us, "Is anything wrong?" And we say "No." "Are you upset?" they ask. And we say, "No." "Do you want to talk?" Certainly not. Sometimes we are that way with God. "Lord, I really have some problems and I need to pray, but I don't want to do it. There are other things that are more important." But sooner or later, and I keep repeating this, sooner or later - you may be in that place now - there will be a crisis or circumstance in your life where the only hope you have is prayer. And the fact is that's the only hope we have all the time; God.

This widow, she kept pressing the judge, until he finally gave in. Now the difference between the judge and God is persistent pressure caused the judge to cave in, and perpetual prayer is the key to activity with God. We don't always change God's mind, because we're not all-knowing, but He changes us as we pray to be in harmony with His will. Even though Jesus said, "He will ask speedily, He doesn't hold off," it is by us constantly praying that we are in tune with and can hear and understand the voice of God.

Prayer stirs the heart of God. And as we draw close to God, and we see His goodness, and He begins to unveil His purpose and plan for our life, that is when our plans begin to fit in their proper place, subject to God's plans; not God being subject to our plans.

He said "God won't delay his answers," verses six through eight. Then the Lord said, "Hear what the unjust judge said, and shall God not avenge His own elect who cry out day and night to Him, though He bears long with them. I tell you that He will avenge them speedily." Nevertheless, when the Son of Man comes will he really find faith on the earth? We can't badger God into an answer. We can't blackmail God into an answer.

Years ago there was a man who said, "I will keep praying until this particular prayer is answered and I won't eat a bite until then." It got into the newspapers. And he literally starved himself to death. Why didn't God answer? You can't threaten God, even with your life. God will do His will, He will accomplish His purpose.

My father's faith can't save me, nor my mother's faith. God has no grandchildren. He just has sons and daughters, and every one of us has a choice to make, and that choice is made when we learn to communicate and to commune with God. And when we pray, God immediately responds. We may not see the answer, we may not agree with the answer. But God hears us the minute we pray. And with the answer, and with fellowship with God, and communion with God, when we get all of the underbrush garbage out of our life, we can hear His voice, we can sense His presence in our spirit, and experience His peace. No matter how difficult or lost or hopeless things may seem.

We lived in Casper, Wyoming. My dad was always starting a church, and by the time it would get big enough to half way support him he would start another one. So we weren't poor, we just didn't have anything. So to have meat he hunted; for those of you who are opposed to that bear with me. Once I went rabbit hunting with my dad. I was in the 3rd grade, just starting the 3rd grade. We were out in the hills of Wyoming and I got tired, so he sent me back to the car. He'd been teaching me right hand, left hand, and I was really proud that I knew them. He said, "Now, Son, you know which is your right hand and which is your left. When you come to this drawer you just go off to your left, and you will be right there in the car. I will be there in a little while."

Well, I was walking along thinking right hand, left hand and right hand... so this became the left hand, so I went on the right, wrong way. And I got lost. It started getting dark, and there's lots of coyotes out there, and they were howling, and I was trying to be manly - whatever that is. It depends on the circumstance. Generally speaking, if we'd be honest, women are tougher than men. We just make a lot of noise. I started crying, "Dad, I'm lost." Then it got evening, and it got dark. I was lost for maybe an hour or so. My dad believed that when you're in the 3rd grade you should be grown up. That was the way he was raised. He was on his own from the 3rd grade. But I will never forget, I was hollering and crying so loud that I didn't hear him come up, I just felt his big old powerful hand reach down and take mine. And I stopped crying. He said, "Son, let's go back to the car."

I was completely at peace. My circumstances as far as where I was hadn't changed; just the fact that my father was there. And that's what happens in prayer. When you finally reach out and sample faith and pray, and you put aside all the barriers that we erect between ourselves and God. And the Bible talks about, "When we seek Him with our whole heart, He will be fond of us." The circumstances when you pray don't outwardly change. The need that you are praying for may even get worse for a while.

The scripture says, "Peace that passes understanding." Why is that? Because there is nothing that you can see that makes you have peace, except the knowledge that God is taking care of it, and He will in His own good time and His own good way, bring it to pass because He loves you. And Jesus said, "When He comes will He find faith on the earth?" He doesn't tell us one way or the other whether there will be faith or not. But He didn't say "If I come back," He said "When I come back." And He will come back.

Martin Luther said, "You that maintain a concern about religion, why don't you pray instead of arguing whether there is a

God or whether there isn't a God or how God does this or God does something else. Don't get into some big theological squabble, just begin to pray. Why don't you just pray?" And God will give you the answer, and God will show you the way.

Lord, we thank you for the access you've given us to yourself. It is such a privilege to come into your magnificent and eternal, all-seeing and all-knowing presence. To not only have fellowship with you but, through your Son Jesus, to be your friend. And Lord, we want to prepare our minds, our spirits, bodies, souls, all of us to be sufficiently in tune with you that we will know your voice and recognize your directions, your instructions, your encouragement, whatever we need you to pour into our lives. And when we ask, we want to ask not according to our will, but according to yours. And we thank you for your Word that guides us into prayer communion with you. Speak to our hearts through the Word today Father, and give us spiritual understanding of what the Spirit would say to the church today. We ask this in the name of our Lord and our Savior, our Friend, our Deliverer Jesus Christ, Amen.

THE UPPER ROOM DISCOURSE

Greater Works Than These

John 14:12-17

We read in the upper room discourse, that Jesus Himself prays for each one of us. Can we grasp it? No. How is God connected through every human being on the face of the earth, and everything that is going beneath the earth, and out in the universe? That's because He is God. There is no place on Heaven or earth that is godforsaken. I have heard people say, "Oh, this is a godforsaken place." No, it's not. He is still there. We forsake Him, He doesn't forsake us. The scripture says He is faithful, even when we're unfaithful. And He loves us, even when we don't love Him, because He can't deny Himself. So this morning we're going to talk about Jesus' prayer for us, and we'll turn to the Book of John 14. In the course of the message this morning we'll go through verses 12 through 17. "Verily, verily, I say unto you, he that believeth on me, the works that I do shall he do also; and greater works than these shall he do; because I go unto my Father."

When I was a little kid my dad did a lot of traveling. He was a superintendent over a number of churches in the State of Wyoming. There would be a long drive between churches, and I would often ride with him when I was about six, seven, eight, nine years old. When I got sleepy and I tried to sleep in the car, he would pester me. He would reach over and he'd grab my leg and I'd say, "Dad, I'm sleepy, turn my leg loose," and he says, "That's not your leg, it's mine." I said, "No it's mine." He said, "Well, you're my son, aren't you?" "Yes!" "Well if you're my son, that's my leg." And this would go on, and go on, and I'd wake up, finally we'd start laughing and have fun.

And when you think about it, when you give your life to Christ, we're talking about your whole life, body, soul and spirit. He takes control of a greater part of your life, and you just become one. It's kind of like when you've been married forty or fifty years. You know, people usually don't get divorced after that. And I know why, because it takes a long time to fully train a husband. It really does. And you know when you lose your old dog and he's adapted to you, and you get a puppy, and you always wonder "Am I going to get another puppy, because puppies are cute but they are a lot of trouble" and that's kind of the way it is with another husband. They might be kind of cute but they're a lot of trouble. It takes a lot of time to train them.

We belong to God. So the work that I do is not mine, it's Christ working in me. And it is Christ's character that enables me to do His activities through my body. We belong to Christ, and now we have this amazing, outrageous statement when Jesus said, "The works that I do if you believe in me, you'll do also. And greater works are these because I go to the Father." If you want to look at it in one sense, as one writer puts it, "When we walk with Christ our activity is borrowed activity." We borrow from Christ what He would do, and He does it through our lives as we yield to Him. We have spiritual authority, but it is not our authority, it's His authority. It is borrowed authority. It doesn't belong to us, it belongs to Christ. And then there is borrowed deity; we're not God, but God takes residence within us to accomplish His work, to fulfill the purpose of His activities.

The reality is, when you give your life to Christ, your activities change. How you spend your time, how you live your life; what you say, what you abstain from saying; what you do, what you abstain from doing. When we fully yield ourselves to Him, Christ becomes the director of our lives, and of our activities. It's important in the scripture to read the instructions that God's given us. When He said "…greater works than He did, you'll do," that sounds preposterous. He raised the dead, He walked on water. He took the blind eyes and touched them and they could see again.

He knew what people were thinking. And what's amazing is, He promised greater works in us.

Now what He is not saying is that as individuals we can do greater works than He did. He's not saying that if we're dedicated enough we can raise the dead, we can open blind eyes. But what He is saying is, that He would do greater works than He did at as the incarnate Christ living among men. Now there's a reason for that. Your mind may be somewhere else, but believe me your body is here, right where you are. And you've got to keep in mind that wherever you go, there you are. You're there, you are limited by your body. I hear about astral projection and all this exotic stuff, you might let your mind drift off somewhere, especially during a long arduous sermon. The fact of the matter is, it doesn't matter. Your mind can go where it wants to - for a few minutes - but we've got your body.

This was the way Christ was. He had the same limitations of the flesh that you and I have. He chose to take them. But when He was on earth, His activity was confined to that human body. He can only be in one place at one time. Thousands of people followed Him, and listened to every word that He said. But He said "I am going to go to the Father, and I'm going to release the full potential of the Godhead that was contained in one human body, and I'm going to take that full potential of the Godhead and release it in the life of every believer." So the presence of Christ in you brings Christ to wherever you are.

There are millions of Christians today carrying out the work of God. They couldn't do that at all if Jesus was still here on earth. Jesus said "It's necessary that I go because if I don't go the Holy Spirit won't come" and work through you. He multiplied Himself in us. So as we yield ourselves, our body and soul to Christ, we bring the Spirit, the presence, the power, the authority of Jesus into other lives; as they are in us, because we don't belong to ourselves anymore, we belong to Christ.

Through our personalities and lives we do greater works in number than He did because there's more of us. But it's not our work, it's His work that is taking place in us. It is the indwelling Christ, the indwelling Spirit. In John 14: 13-14 He said, "In whatever you ask in my name that will I do, that the Father may be glorified in the Son. If you ask anything in my name I will do it." Now here is the condition, that the Father maybe glorified in the Son. You say "Okay I'll just ask for a new car, or a new house, or a new refrigerator, whatever." Sometimes God blesses us with those things, but that's not the authority He's talking about. He's talking about things that God desires us to do through our lives when we totally yield and respond to the promptings of the Holy Spirit. Things that will glorify God.

Now there is authorized, and unauthorized, activity. You remember the sons of Sceva in the Books of Acts. They watched Jesus and Paul cast out demons and deliver people. And so they started, the seven sons of Sceva said alright, "That's a good gig, we're going to go cast out demons." So they went over to this demon possessed man, and all seven of them said, "In the name of whatever, we command you to come out." And the guy looked at them, and the demon said, "Jesus I know and Paul I know, but who are you?" And he just beat those guys. They were terrified, because their power couldn't match the power of demons.

You say, "What did Jesus do?" He would say "Come out." And what do we do? "In the name or by the authority of Jesus Christ we command you to come out." That's not us who's doing it, don't ever think it is. It's Christ in us. This is what the scripture is talking about, this authority that God gives us. This spiritual authority. Lord, we bind these spiritual powers that come against us, in the name of Jesus.

Now you and I as human beings are no match for the Devil, or even the most junior demon. Mary and I have witnessed things of demonic power that would stagger the imagination. We've witnessed some in this country, here it is a little more subtle, and a little more covered up, but in some of the places where we lived, South America, Africa, and the Middle East we saw things happen.

I saw something one night that just shocked me. I was preaching in a soccer stadium in Rio de Janeiro, 30-40,000 people were there. I don't know how long a soccer field is because I'm not interested in soccer. So, I started preaching, and all of a sudden there was a commotion out on the field packed with people. Suddenly people started falling back, and there was this guy on his sides, slithering and writhing down the length of the whole soccer field at lightning speed. And a young Brazilian pastor jumped off the platform, who was about half again as tall as the man on the ground, and ran out on the field screaming out. I don't know how his voice was amplified in that crowd but I could hear him. He said to that demon, "I know you - in the name of Jesus Christ come out," and that man quieted down; the snake-like convulsions propelling him across the field stopped. They helped him up. The missionary with us said they always send that particular pastor to demon possessed people, he has a special gift. He wasn't doing it in his authority.

Dramatic things like that, maybe they don't happen too often. But there are spiritual forces that fight us every day and we have the authority when Christ is living in us to overcome and defeat those spiritual powers Satan would bring against us. We are not a captive to him. If you trust in God, and you walk and live in the Spirit, recognize this; your enemy is already defeated. When you come to Christ, Satan has no power over you. Why? Because Christ in you has the authority over the enemy. And there is nothing that comes against you that is greater than the power of a living Christ within you. We have that borrowed authority that God places in us, when we yield ourselves to Jesus Christ.

God said in John 15:15, "You didn't choose me, I chose you and appointed you that you should go and bear fruit and that your fruit should remain." One of the things that thrills me, is when I run into people who say, "I used to go to your church." Most of them are still serving the Lord, they're in other churches, in other places. I've never gone to the East Coast, at conferences or wherever I speak, without running into somebody who found Christ at the Warehouse. They're scattered all over and it thrills me, because the fruit remains.

This what Christ prays for us. We have His authority working in us, and whatever we ask in His name, that He will I do. So we work in His name on the conditions that we've been talking about this morning. Our life and service to God is followed with 'greater works' because we borrow His deity. We're not God, we're not Christ, and this is the appeal to the arrogance of the human spirit. Many of the religions of the world tell us that if we go through certain things, and do certain things we become God. Some even say that Jesus went through all of the sacrifice and work and He became God, and in the same way that Jesus became God, you can ultimately become God. But the Bible tells us that there's only the Father, Son, and Holy Spirit; the three in one. One God. And when people start telling you, "You can be God," they're not telling the truth.

But what we have is God in us, the living God, the powerful God who is the Holy Spirit who is in constant communion with Jesus. Jesus said it's necessary that I go away because if not He says, the Spirit of truth can't come. He can come after I'm glorified. So let's look at it John 14:15-17, "If ye love me, keep my commandments. And I will pray the Father, and he shall give you another Comforter, that he may abide with you for ever. Even the Spirit of truth; whom the world cannot receive, because it seeth him not, neither knoweth him: but ye know him; for he dwelleth with you, and shall be in you."

As we yield to the Holy Spirit our power and authority operates according to need. There's a lot of Christians going to Heaven, but they are not living in the power and authority of God. They haven't let the Spirit come in and take possession and control of our lives. When the Holy Spirit comes into your life it gives you spiritual strength, spiritual authority, spiritual power, spiritual force. The Holy Spirit works through our lives bringing special gifts for special needs. So the Brazilian pastor is given the power to confront the demon in the moment of need. "Greater is He that is in us than he that is in the world," greater than the forces that oppose us is the Holy Spirit.

I'm going to share this message someday of great men of God who served the Lord and worked for God. Men like Dwight L.

Moody, Charles Finny and a number of others who were praying, "God we need more of your power and presence in our lives, Lord we want learn to yield to you." And they would pray and they would seek God. They had these incredible spiritual experiences they wrote about, and their ministries and their lives changed, dramatically and radically forever

What happens when the Holy Spirit comes into our lives? First of all we know the truth. He unfolds and open our eyes to reality. He exposes error. He tears away the veil of confusion and unbelief. He removes spiritual blindness. He removes doubts about God. He gives us the power and the courage to face the realities of life. The world is blinded to the Spirit, and many Christians are not walking and living in the Spirit. He is with them, but they've never really said, "Holy Spirit come into my life, immerse me in your presence, baptize me afresh, baptize me anew." What happened to the disciples, they received the Spirit's baptism in Acts Chapter 2, and we find them a short time later praying again that God would renew them in the Spirit. Because life, and the realities of life, and the pressures of life, wear away our consciousness of God.

He said the world cannot receive Him, they can't see Him, if it doesn't know Him. "But you know Him for He dwells with you and will be in you. I will not leave you orphans. I will come to you in the dwelling of the Father and the Son a little while longer and the world will see me no more, but you will see me; because I live, you will live also." So Jesus is saying, when the Spirit comes and infuses you, then the work that I do you're going to do. And He is actually praying for us, that we would respond and receive the Holy Spirit that we might continue the work that Christ began. And that we might become His representatives.

Lord, we thank you for your presence, we thank you for the promises that you've given us. We thank you for your faithfulness, for Lord you never tell us something that's isn't true. So many lies, so many distortions, but Lord you are truth. And we thank you for giving us access Lord, to you and to your Heavenly Kingdom, and our Heavenly Father, and to the Holy Spirit. So open our hearts to receive what the Spirit would say to us. And I pray that anyone, Lord, whatever circumstances closed the door of their heart to you, may they open it today and invite you in. The handle is on the inside Lord, and only we can invite you in. No one can do it for us. I pray this will happen; that the fulfillment and the peace that we all seek and never find without you, shall be made very real to every heart here today. We pray this in Jesus' name. Amen.

KEPT IN CHRIST

Able to Keep You From Falling
John 17: 9 -19

This morning I'm going to share something that's very near to me, and that is the fact that Jesus prays for us. Our Savior prays for us. I'd like to focus your attention on ten verses of scripture, John 17:9-19. Although I don't usually do this, I want to read the whole text.

John tells us Jesus is praying to the Father, saying, "I pray for them: I pray not for the world, but for them which you have given me; for they are yours. And all mine are thine, and thine are mine; and I am glorified in them. And now I am no more in the world, but these are in the world, and I come to you. Holy Father, keep through thine own name those whom thou hast given me, that they may be one, as we are. While I was with them in the world, I kept them in thy name: those that thou gavest me I have kept, and none of them is lost, but the son of perdition; that the scripture might be fulfilled. And now come I to thee; and these things I speak in the world, that they might have my joy fulfilled in themselves. I have given them thy Word; and the world has hated them, because they are not of the world, even as I am not of the world. I pray not that thou shouldest take them out of the world, but that thou shouldest keep them from evil. They are not of the world, even as I am not of the world. Sanctify them through thy truth: thy word is truth. As thou have sent me into the world, even so have I also sent them into the world. And for their sakes I sanctify myself, that they also might be sanctified through the truth."

Sometimes we get so wrapped up in the beauty, in the poetic nature of Jesus' language, that we miss this powerful prayer that prepares us to live in this world and to glorify Him. We'll be considering what the scripture means when it talks about 'the world' in just a little while later in this message, but first, shall we pray.

Father, thank you for your Word, thank you for your love for us, for the gift of your son Jesus, for the Holy Spirit that you have sent to be with us continually and to commune and communicate with us and through us. And thank you for giving us the mission of sharing with others who don't know you and the joy, the fulfillment, the satisfaction that can be found only in a full surrender of our lives to the Savior, Jesus Christ. Speak to us today, we pray in Jesus' name, and may we listen and hear. And may the Word be applied to our lives, that we might continue, and even in a greater measure to glorify you by the way we live through your power. We ask this in Jesus' name, Amen.

This prayer was offered by the Lord just before He went into the garden of Gethsemane, before He went to the judgment seat of Pilate, before He suffered such terrible indignities of pain - body, soul and spirit - as He prepared to go to the cross. And as He was praying this prayer, the disciples had the feeling that Jesus was leaving them. And they were bereft. They were just feeling a real sense of loss, because their whole life for the years they had been with Him was wrapped up in being in fellowship with Him. They had been witnessing His love, His compassion, and His power, and sharing in His ministry with the needy people they constantly came in contact with.

But now, as He gave this prayer, they begun to sense that he was leaving them, and that they would remain. And they didn't yet understand why it was necessary. Jesus Himself said, "It is necessary that I go away. If I don't go the Spirit can't come, and when the Spirit comes, then He won't talk about Himself. What He hears of me He will share with you. And you will have an even closer and greater connection with me by the Holy Spirit, than you had with me when I walked among you in the flesh." They did not yet understand that. And so Jesus, going back to the 11th verse of John 17, said, "Now I'm no longer in the world, but these are in the world, and I come to you Holy Father, keep through your name those whom you have given me, that they maybe one as we are." I suppose if there would be a title to the message, or a theme of the message, it would be 'Kept in Christ', or 'Kept by Christ'. Christ keeps us from something, and saves us for something, and we'll be talking about that in the course of the message this morning.

Christ's priority was to keep them. He said "I didn't lose one that you gave me," and Father I'm trusting you, I'm asking you bless them, keep them. It's one thing to start out on a journey; it's another to finish it. It's one thing to take a few steps towards an objective; it's another that, no matter how difficult and arduous the task and the trail might be, we accomplish the goal, we reach the end of the journey. "Keep them Lord." There are so many that start out strong, and falter. It doesn't mean that God gives up on them, and that they won't ultimately make the goal - which is heaven. But when we go away from Christ, or grow less than fully committed to Christ, it is such a great loss both to us and to the world that God sent us to. There's one thing you can never recapture once it's misspent or lost; and that's time. Time is precious.

They asked Bill Gates, "What do you lack, what is in it in your life that you don't have enough of now?" And he was talking at the time when he was worth billions and billions of dollars, and had great influence, as he probably still does. He looked at them and gave a one word answer, "One thing I don't have enough of, is time." When we walk away from God, and we walk out of God's will, away from His purpose, we lose that time. And we can never recapture it.

So Jesus is saying, "Father keep them," don't let them stray. Don't let them lose this valuable place of service and ministry that you have reserved for them by taking detours and walking away from your purpose, your reason for their existence. When we're away from our families we pray for them, and we say "Lord take care of my family in my absence." We pray for our families every day, but when we're separated by time and distance, there's that special prayer; Lord keep them. Don't let anything bad happen to them, Lord, keep your hand upon them. We should pray like that all the time. But when we're separated it seems even more poignant, and more pressing.

He prays for us to keep in contact with the Father. Did you know that you can be a Christian and lose contact with God? You can be married and lose contact with your husband or wife; you live in the same house, sleep in the same bed, eat at the same table, and yet completely lose contact until you don't even know each other anymore. And then you begin to wonder why things are crumbling. Suddenly, you begun to live two separate lives, two separate people, not one as God intended; not bound together in the bonds of love. And then suddenly you're shocked when the whole relationship begins to disintegrate, and the comfort and the strength and the joy is gone. And the same thing can happen with us in our relationship with God; we can neglect and put other things before God, until we lose our consciousness of who He is. Because we have a barrage of experiences, and words, and images, blasted into our consciousness every day of our life in this culture. And if we're not careful we can be so filled with things that have no value, that the greatest treasure God ever gave us - which is Himself - is buried. Put into a secondary role, or third role, or completely pushed out of our lives.

Keep them Father. When I drive around my neighborhood occasionally, I'm amazed at the soccer mania. I look at parents, and their whole life is planned around their kids' schedule. Their time is devoted. There are people that are counting on little Junior or little Suzie becoming a star athlete, become world famous, so that the parents can bask in the glory, and receive financial benefits in their old age. We invest our lives, and how many of those kids make it? Of all the guys I played football with, only two of them ever turned professional. And they weren't very successful. But when we played they were king. And yet we invest our lives in so many things; we have hobbies, we have distractions, we have diversions.

In the 14th and 15th verses of John 17, let's say it again, "I've given them your Word, and the world has hated them, because they are not of the world, just as I am not of the world. I do not pray that you should take them out of the world, but that you should keep them from evil."

Have you ever listened to the newscast when some of these so called sophisticated people are discussing Christians? It's usually a pretty derogatory conversation; not always, but often. How many times in a movie have you seen a dedicated, committed born again Christian portrayed as somebody of value and character, somebody to be emulated and admired? It happens, but it's rare. And as Christians we shouldn't expect it; because when we were away from the Lord we were not all that gung-ho for gung-ho Christians. We avoided them as best we could, we made fun of them. At least I did.

I was listening to the radio the other day, and the sportscaster was rejoicing in the fact that he's proposing to his bosses to have a radio program sponsored by them on a pay for listen station. And here are the reasons he wants to do that; so he can use unbridled profanity, and talk about all sorts of things in relationship to women and politics, and everything else. And, he said, to make fun of people.

Christians, the Bible said, are the restraining force in the world. So there is opposition. Jesus says it, He tells us; don't expect the world to like you. Don't expect non-Christians to rejoice in your salvation and your righteousness. You're a hindrance. The Bible says, we are the salt of the earth, we are the light of the world. We are holding back the final corruption, and when the church is taken out of the world, this world will literally disintegrate into anarchy and chaos. And it's on the brink of it right now. There's so much anger, there's so much hatred in this world, and so much violence.

The problem is that wherever you go, there you are. It doesn't make any difference. Whatever is in your heart, whatever is in your life, if you carry it with you there's not an environment that will change you; the only thing that can change it is to enter into the presence of God and fully commit your life to Jesus Christ. Because behind the world, with all its deceptions, and all its tricks, and all its appeal, is a mastermind called the Devil. And the demonic forces are highly organized, divided up into the various sections of his kingdom throughout the world. What is his purpose? Jesus said, "I have come that you might life and have it more abundantly;" but the enemy, the Devil, has come to steal, to kill and to destroy. But He has come that you might have life; not just existence, but an abundant, rich life, and a full life.

So the definition of the world is a philosophy that people can live, and be fulfilled, and fulfill their purpose in life without God. And politically, Christians who believe that God's Word is true, that people will live healthier and happier lives, and families will be stronger, and children will raise up with a greater hope if they follow the teachings of Christ; we're now called social conservatives. Social conservatives. What we're trying to conserve is the joy, the peace, and the purpose that Christ died on the cross to bring to every human being on the face of the earth. We won't do it politically; it will take place in the spiritual change. The world says the problem is Christians. If you don't believe that, talk to any college student. They will tell you the problem in the world is Christians.

How are we kept? In the first verse of John 17, Jesus spoke these words; He lifted up His eyes into the heaven, and He said, "Father, the hour has come; glorify your son that your son also may glorify you." Jesus wants to be glorified in your life, that you will become a beacon of love and light and hope to the people in the world around you. It's been my experience that people who don't want to talk to me, who have been in church and gone away from the Lord, I've actually seen them go four isles out of the way in a grocery store to miss me. I saw it just a week ago; I tracked him down anyway, but it didn't make any difference. Why? Some of these same people when a crisis comes, guess who they call? They may get off into all kinds of strange religions, or shallow surface religions... but when it comes to time for a funeral of a family member, the phone rings. And when there's a marriage breaking up, when a child is sick, when a disease attaches itself to a body, where do you turn? You turn to whoever it is in your life that reflects the presence, the power and the hope of Jesus Christ.

"I've given them your Word, and the world hated them because they are not of the world, just as I am not of the world. I do not pray that you should take them out of the world, but that you keep them from evil." God wants to preserve you; God's desire is to keep you. Jesus' prayer for you, is that you not lose out, that you don't begin the race and not finish it; that you don't walk in discouragement and defeat rather than the victory and power that He purchased for you. But He didn't stay on the cross. The cross is empty. He is risen from the dead. And He sits in all power and glory, at the right hand of God, and God himself is praying for you.

What is there in our lives that He can't overcome? There's nothing too hard for the Lord. There's nothing too difficult for the Lord, period. The world has said the problem is Christians, and that's just not true. The hope is Christians; the hope is Christ. And Jesus spoke this word and lifted up His eyes to heaven and said, "Glorify your son, that your son may also glorify you." He says, "I am kept and in your name those you gave me, I have kept and none of them are lost, except the son of perdition." We can't do it on our own, and the scripture teaches us that.

In the Book of 2 Timothy 1:12, "For this reason I also suffer these things: nevertheless I am not ashamed, for I know whom I have believed, and am persuaded that He is able to keep that which I have committed unto Him against that day." I know of my imperfections, and I know of my sins; and I've repented, and I ask God daily for forgiveness and cleansing. I know what a rotten person I am without Christ, what a selfish person I can be without Jesus. I know those things. But I also know His power. And I'm persuaded that when I give myself to Him, He will defeat the evil and the sin, and bring His righteousness, and holiness, and purity, and love, and generosity into my life. I can represent Him, because He is able to keep what I have committed unto him against that day. What have I committed? I've committed my life, my eternity, my soul, every part of my being belongs to Him. Now I want to honor Him.

We're kept by the power of God. 1 Peter 1:5 says, "Who are kept by the power of God through faith for salvation ready to be revealed in the last time." You say "But I can't make it." Yes you can. Don't get that attitude, "Oh I think I've tried this, I've followed the Lord, I've given up, it hasn't worked." How many times have I heard that? How many times have I said that? I've done it all right. You say, "Wait a minute; I've raised my kids right, they're going through all kinds of stuff." You did your part. God said when they are older, at some point in their life, they're going to come back. They will look a little shop worn and beat up, but they'll come back. You said, "But how do you know that?" Because I have seen lots of you come back. You look pretty shop worn and beat up, but God saved you, and renewed you, and you start over again.

That's the joy, that's the joy that take place in our lives. We can't do it on our own, though. 2 Timothy 1:12 says "For this reason I also suffer these things: nevertheless I am not ashamed, for I know whom I have believed, and am persuaded that He is able to keep that which I have committed unto that day." Remember that scripture, go over it again and again.

Peter talks about these things; we are kept by the power of God, not by our strength, but the power of God in our lives. The working of the Holy Spirit. Now, who is able to keep us? Jesus. Jude 24 said - there's only one chapter in Jude, it's not a chapter it's a book, one book without a chapter - it said, "Now take Him who is able to keep you from stumbling, and to present you faultless before the presence of His glory with exceeding joy." He will keep you, He will preserve you. He is able to keep you through the power of God and to present you faultless in the presence of Jesus.

Now there was one exception; his name was Judas. John 17:12; "While I was with them in the world, I have kept them and none of them is lost, except the son of perdition." The fact is, Judas never submitted the inner man to Christ. He was a devout and deeply religious man, he was a follower of the law, but he also thought he could move in on what Christ was doing, for his own benefit. He believed strongly that Jesus was going to establish His kingdom on earth and that if he would follow Him, he would be a part of the ruling party. And when he began to realize that the kingdom wasn't of this earth, he sold Him out because he was dissolute. I have a friend that I've prayed for for years; he is very, very old now. But he was such a student of prophecy in the Book of Daniel, and he thought he had it all figured out. How God was going to come, and when he was going to come. But when it didn't happen, he lost his faith. I told him, "You didn't have faith in Jesus; you had faith in your ability to interpret Biblical prophecy." Because the Bible said no man knows the day or the hour. But he is still struggling, in his ninety first year of life, and I still pray for him that he'll come back.

It is Jesus that we look to. Judas never made an inner surrender of his heart to Christ, he never fully submitted. Peter said in John 6:68, "But Simon answered and said, Lord, to whom shall we go?" You have the word of eternal life. Where shall we go but to Jesus. You have the word of eternal life. There's no one else that died again in perfect innocence, and rose from the dead on the third day, and ascended into the heavens. There's no one else Lord, if we don't have you; where do we go from there? Do we go to Buddha, do we go to Krishna, do we go to Muhammad? No, no one else. There's no one else that did or can do what Jesus did; because He was not a man searching for God, He was God revealing himself in the flesh. And making it possible through His forgiveness and His power, to cleanse, to give us access into the holy, righteous, and pure presence of God the Father.

Sanctify them by your truth. Your Word is truth and you sent me into the world. I also have sent them into the world, and for their sakes, I sanctify myself, that they also may be sanctified by the truth. Sometimes we look at the word 'sanctification' and we say; what in the world is that? Sanctification has a very simple definition. If you are sanctified it means that you are put to your proper use, to be set apart and made holy for His service. Jesus came and was put to His proper use, to live a sinless life, to die on the cross; that's the use, that's the purpose. Sanctification. What is our proper use? It is to walk in fellowship with God; to let Jesus live His life through us; to empower us by the Holy Spirit to bear witness and to bring people to that turning point in life. That is the ultimate purpose of every Christian's life.

The purpose of God in the world is to give every man and woman, through the Word of God, through an intelligent presentation of the Word of God, an opportunity to accept or reject Jesus Christ. That's what God placed us here for. Satan would like you to say, "Well, things are so tough" ….and you start looking back, romanticizing how wonderful things were back then. It's like the Children of Israel; "We had it so good in Egypt, here we are out in this desert and everything stinks. Yeah, I know they were taking our baby boys and killing them. I know we were slaves and being beaten with whips and underfed. I know we were miserable and complaining to God, wanting out of there, and He sent us out. But I don't like where he put us. Egypt looks really good. Ha, if I could just have some garlic and some onions, and a little spice. Manna, manna, manna, I'm tired of manna, I can't stand any more manna, I've had enough grape nut flakes to last me forever." That's the closest thing we have to what manna was.

Things weren't any good at all when we were away from the Lord. It's just a lie of the enemy. You say "I can't make it, I can't hang on." Yes you can, you can. "For greater is He that is in you, than he that is in the world." And all the love and power that Jesus has, is poured out upon us when we fulfill the purpose for which He created us. Our purpose is to live and walk in this world, and to reveal through our lives the message of redemption and the love that God has for the whole human race.

Father, thank you for your Word, thank you for your love for us, for the gift of your son Jesus, for the Holy Spirit that you have sent to be with us, continually to commune and communicate with us and through us. Keep us from temptation and evil. Keep us from our own faithlessness and doubt. May we trust you to perfect us and preserve us. We ask this in Jesus' name, Amen.

PURPOSE OF PRAYER

Mission of the Church
John 17:20-26

There is a very specific mission that God has called the church to fulfill, but much of Christianity has been diverted from that overriding objective. And this is what we'll be talking about in the course of today's sermon. We're going to read several verses this morning, John Chapter 17, verses 20 through 26. This is a vital prayer that Christ offered just prior to the crucifixion. It was His last time in prayer with the disciples before Calvary. Jesus was praying, and He said, "I do not pray for these alone," speaking of His disciples, "But also for those who will believe in me through their word. That they may all be one, as you Father are in me, and I in you, and they also may be one in us. That the world may believe that you sent me, and the glory which you gave me, I have given them that they may be one; just as we are one, I in them and you in me, that they may be made perfect in one. And that the world may know that you have sent me, because you have loved them as you have loved me.

Father, I desire that they also, whom you gave me, may be with me, where I am, that they may behold my glory which you have given me. For you loved me before the foundations of the world. Oh righteous Father, the world doesn't know you, but I have known you; and these have known that you sent me. And I have declared to them your name, and will declare it. That the love with which you love me may be in them, and I in them."

This is the prayer that Jesus left with the disciples before he went to Calvary. And He speaks to us distinctly of the mission of the church through prayer. This mission can only be fulfilled as we pray, and come in contact with God. The last meeting with His disciples ended with this particular prayer meeting, and Jesus led the prayer meeting Himself. What a prayer meeting that must have been. He still leads prayer meetings through His Holy Spirit. He still guides and directs the path of our prayers, as we open our hearts to Him. We can look at this as the last gathering; the Father, the Son and the Holy Spirit have a summit. They talk about the fact that they will share their mission, and the purpose of God sending Jesus to earth, to carry this message through the disciples to a needy world.

Their plan is for all time, between the Cross and the Second Coming. It is for every human being that ever existed, who exists now, or will exist. This is the prayer that God has for every human being that was ever born or conceived. First of all He established a goal. Secondly, a strategy - an overview of how to accomplish the goal. And finally tactics - specific maneuvers that explain how to reach the goal, to see the plan come to full fruition.

"So that the world believes that you have sent me." Twice in these six verses, Jesus makes this statement; first in verse 21, and again in verse 23. "So that the world may know that you have sent me." This is the mission of the church; to let the world know that God sent Jesus Christ to redeem us from our sins, and to bring us into fellowship with God, so that God might take residence in the core of our literal being.

The Bible teaches us that our body is the temple of the Holy Spirit, the dwelling place of God. Our soul is our mind, our will, our intellect and our spirit. These are the places that God desires to live in us; to cohabit with us in our spirit and in our lives. Through our spirit-filled lives, the world may know that God has revealed Himself through His Son Jesus Christ.

God's redemptive plan is aimed at the whole world. We've quoted it many times in this series on prayer, John 3:16; "For God so loves the world." It's easy for us to forget that. Jesus said, "I pray not that you take them out of the world but that you keep them from evil." He said, "Go therefore into all the world and declare the good news of God's love and redemption to every creature."

I've never been inspired to do it, but I hear of cruises where it's all Christians. So we preach to each other. We go out and we get on these cruises, and I saw a brochure saying which celebrity is going too. Every day on the cruise they will have a Bible study on how to reach the world. Here we are on this ship, and here is the world out there dying. Sounds like I'm dogging it, but I'm really not, it's just such a strange thing.

What the Devil would like is for us is to be so fearful of the world we hide from it, we isolate ourselves from the very mission that Jesus called us to fulfill. We need to have contact with, and be friends with people who do not yet know Jesus that they might see the love that God has placed in our hearts for every human being. Through our love they will see God has prepared for them to come into fellowship with their Creator, though the sacrifice of Jesus Christ. God loves them. God cares for them. God's not mad at them all the time. God loves us, and we are the ones Jesus said who are to reflect that message to the world. And yet as Christians we all have such a tendency to hide from those who don't agree with us, to not be a part of the world that we live in. To isolate and separate ourselves. And this is exactly contrary to the prayer that Jesus prayed for us.

"Christians in the world," Jesus said; I want you to be in the world, but not of the world. I want you to be different. I want them to see a genuine love, a genuine compassion, a genuine care for the world that we live in. Christians have a purpose being in this world. And it's tragic, but many believers, earnest, sincere people, divert the emphasis of the message God intended us to carry out. I guess what I'm going to say may sound controversial to you, but I just encourage you to think about it. We are not here to improve the world; we are not here to make social and political changes; we are here for but one thing - to fulfill our ultimate mission. Our ultimate mission. We are here not to improve or save the world, we are here for one purpose, and I share it again; "that they may all be one, as you Father are in me, and I in you; that they also may be one in us, that the world may believe that you sent me."

He doesn't say "God so loved the church." He does love the Church, but He loves the world. He died for the world. And you and I, every one of us were in the world and under the wrath God, until we came into a relationship with Jesus. And that's our mission.

There is quite a popular thing going on right now that has a kind of loosely defined word called 'social justice'. The idea is to bring economic justice and equality to all human beings in the world, through political and social means, and also the church should get on board. There's nothing wrong with some of those things. But that's not our mission. Our mission is to show the world that God sent Jesus to reveal Himself to human beings. And the only way we can make the case is to truly be born of God, and filled with His love for the world that we live in. His compassion. John 17; "He carries out this purpose that God wants us to fulfill."

I was reading a commentary the other day, and there was a pastor that was at a missionary conference. And in the conference they were asking the missionaries to define world evangelism. What does world evangelism mean to you? This particular pastor said there was one thing that really struck his heart. And I quote; "World evangelism is the attempt to get every man an opportunity to make an intelligent choice to receive or reject Jesus Christ."

That's what God sent us to do, by our living in the world, but not being of the world, by being filled with the Holy Spirit, the love of God reaches out through us. Yes, the church will continue to try to minister to people and help provide food for the hungry. We do those things, but that's not our primary mission. It's tragic when people are clothed and fed and still spiritually void, for their end is unchanged unless they come to Jesus Christ. All of these things are fine, but that's not our primary mission. Our primary mission is to give men and women an opportunity to make an intelligent choice to receive the Word of God. To receive Jesus Christ into their lives and to be transformed. To receive Him or reject Him. God has given every human being that ability to choose.

We can't do it sitting on the sidelines; being isolated from the world that we live in, and from people who are in the world but who have not yet received Jesus. How many of you, let me ask, how many of you were made conscious of your need of Christ though some friend, who by his life or his witness influenced your life? Could I see your hands this morning? Somebody spoke to you. Somebody talked to you. But as the church matures, we get uncomfortable with the world.

Mary and I were having dinner at a restaurant, and right behind us was a couple who were really drunk, and loud and boisterous. Just listening to them you realize what a miserable life they have together. She said, "You haven't said anything nice to me in twenty years, you know," and he said, "Blankety blank, I have said nice blankety blank things to you." This is in a restaurant, loud voices and a lot of lubrication, so they were talking and I just sat there and listened a little bit. Well you didn't have a choice really, you either get up and give up and walk out and have to pay for the dinner I didn't eat, or whatever. But I just sat there and listened to them, everybody in the restaurant listened to them, but the fact of the matter is that I just sat there and said, "Lord somehow reach those people." They are miserable. They have a miserable life. Can you imagine living with somebody, first that thinks they are unloved, and second that the other curses her out to prove he loves her? You know, it's a different modus operandi I have. It was amazing.

So this is our mission, this is what God has called us to do. We must not cringe in fear from the world and isolate ourselves from the world. That's why we have a mission here at the Warehouse, and our mission is to manifest the genuine love and concern for humanity that Jesus Christ has given us. When we say to somebody, "How are you doing?" don't just pass it out, but be willing to listen to the answer. And say "Is there something I can do for you" or "I'll pray for you," or "Don't give up hope, God loves you." Whatever God needs you to say, He will give you the right words at the right time. And the scripture says, don't worry about what to say because in that moment when you open your mouth suddenly the Holy Spirit will have the right thing for you to say, if you trust Him and walk in Him.

"That you all may be one." He's not talking about organizational structure; He's talking about oneness of hearts, oneness of life, oneness of purpose. I have a love for all Christians. I don't care much what their doctrine is, as long as they believe in Jesus Christ, and Him being crucified as being the only access to God through forgiveness of our sins, by accepting the sacrifice and the invitation of Jesus Christ to come in to Him. I don't care about these little doctrinal squabbles that have been going on for 2,000 years. They go clear back to the early church. I don't care what you believe about the rapture. I don't care if you believe there's going to be a pre-tribulation rapture (which of course is the right answer) or a mid-tribulation rapture, or a rapture at the end of the tribulation. If you don't agree with me, fine. I don't care, I am not going to waste five minutes arguing with you about the rapture. All I can tell you is this; you are going to be in for a pleasant surprise. You're not going to be here for the tribulation, but that's alright if you want to stay, ask God to leave you behind, that's fine. It's not up to me to test your faith.

I don't care if you believe you were once saved, always saved or never sure you're saved. I don't care about that. I care that you know Jesus, and that you know He loves you. I've got a whole library full of books written by brilliant, godly men, and I don't even read them anymore. I don't care what they have to say anymore. They've said some good things, and I've read most of them over the years; thankfully I've forgotten most of it. What I care about is that people will see us and know that we love God, and God loves us, and that God manifest and reveals His love for them through our eyes. That's what I care about. That's what God cares about.

So how do we accomplish this? In the 24th verse, "Father I desire that they also whom you gave me may be with me where I am, and that they may behold my glory that you have given me. For you have loved me from before the foundations of the world." You say "Well, that verse is talking about heaven." No, it's not. It's talking about right now. Ephesians 2, Jesus said, "We are now seeded in heavenly places." We're with Him right now. We are carrying out His mission. He is with us. He said, "Lo, I am with you always until I go to heaven." No. He said, "Even to the end of the age, I am there, I am with you." You're a part of me, I am a part of you. Heaven is not going to be a huge shock for you. It might be a shock that you made it, but you will know what happened. You will see the continuation in heaven of what you were experiencing on earth.

I will see the same Savior who is within me face to face when I stand in His presence. I will see and recognize the glory and majesty of the Father who has blessed me, and covered me throughout the course of my life. And the Holy Spirit will continue to show me the marvels and wonders of Jesus, and I will fall on my face and say, "Lord, thank you for saving me." And He will reach down like He did to John, He will pick me up and say, "Alright boy, you're okay now, you made it. You made it the minute you gave your life to me and invited me into your soul and into your spirit."

John 5:2 said, "By this we know that we loved the children of God when we love God and keep his commandments." Now God didn't say "If it suits you I want you to love everybody." If you call yourself a Christian, and there is somebody in your life that you won't speak to, you've got a serious sin problem. I am not saying you will lose your soul, but the blessings of God will be withheld from your life until you humble yourself and go to that person and say "Forgive me, I have not had any love in my heart for you, but God touched me and I can repent my sins." And if they look at you and say, "Well you should have done it you know, because you've done some terrible things to me," don't restart the battle. The Bible said, "As far as it depends on you or I, live in peace with all men." You can't do anything about that, but you can be free from any bondage. Any time you have ill will or hatred towards any person, you're the one that's in bondage. And Christ came to set you free.

The absence of love. The scripture says in Romans 12:9, "He said, but let love be without hypocrisy. Abhor what is evil, cling to what is good." Don't have a hypocritical love; just a surface love, where you just kind of smile - in the South everybody loves each other. And they all like to hug, you know, they like to put their arm around you and hug you, "Oh brother Louis, Oh sister Mary. We just love you so much." But you know in their heart that if they had their way they'd pull up a Mike Tyson on you, they'd bite part of your ear off and spit it out on the ground. And you can love that person; theirs isn't sincere, but yours can be.

And that is the witness to the church, when you love them. When you love those that hate you, when you do good to those who spitefully use you, when you return good for evil, and when you forgive - even when forgiveness is not sought by the one who is offended. This is the spirit of Jesus that touches the world and reaches out and embraces the world. There is no exclusiveness. Matthew 5:47, "If you greet your brother only, what do you more than others, do not even tax collectors do that?"

We need to recognize that we need each other. Every Christian who loves Jesus and invited Him into our hearts - they're my brother, they're my sister, and I love every one of them. We may have doctrinal differences. We all manage to find something to fuss over. But I love the brethren and the sisters in Christ. I want the world to know that I love them. You know, my dad used to irritate me; I loved him so much, and then I realized that again, he was right. When he was in a little town of Temple Texas, and had been unable to continue pastoring, but he spent several years continuing living in that town. He loved to go to the cafeteria there at the mall. And when I was there visiting, I would always go to the cafeteria. And I am telling you the truth, it would be like a one hundred yard walk, and it would take a half hour to forty minutes to get to the cafeteria. You know I felt like attacking a snack on the way to lunch. Why? Because every person he saw he talked to.

You care about people you don't even know, and you witness to them, and this is true evangelism. This is the mission of the church. We will not restore the world, let me tell you; Jesus already told us how the world's going to end. He said there's going to be chaos and wars and rumors of wars, men's hearts failing them for fear looking on the things that are coming on the earth. He said there will be anarchy, there will be violence, there will be strife and struggle; we are not going to restore the world because Jesus already told us. If you don't believe it read Luke 21 and Matthew 24, go back and read the Book of Daniel and you'll see. We know how the world is going to end. So in the meantime our overriding mission; yes we do these things, we provide food, we provide clothing and we show them we do that, but that is not what wins the world to Jesus Christ. It is showing the love of God, by looking people in the eye, and really loving, and really caring for them. And only the Holy Spirit can accomplish that in anybody's life.

I want to share with you the philosophy and ministry of Warehouse Christian Ministries and my pastor Chuck Smith of Calvary Chapel. I want you to just look at it and read it while I read it to you this morning. This is a statement of faith.

"Warehouse Christian Ministries has been formed as a fellowship of believers in the Lordship of Jesus Christ. Our supreme desire is to know Christ and to be conformed to His image by the power of the Holy Spirit. We are a non-denominational church, but we are not opposed to denomination, only their tendency to over emphasize the doctrine of differences that have led to the division of the body of Christ. We believe that the only true basis of Christian fellowship is His love, which is greater than any difference we may have. And without His love we have no right to claim ourselves to be Christians. We believe worship of God should be spiritual, therefore we remain flexible and yielded to the leading of the Holy Spirit to direct our worship. Worship of God should be inspirational, therefore we give great place to music in our worship. Worship of God should be intelligent, therefore our services are designed with great emphasis on the teaching of the Word of God, that He might instruct us how He should be worshipped. Worship of God is fruitful, therefore we look for His love in our lives as the supreme manifestation that we have truly been worshiping Him. And that is what we believe."

And that is what Jesus prayed for, and that's what we must pray for in our own lives. So as we pray, let us pattern our prayer life after the prayers of Jesus. The Lord's Prayer; let's pattern our lives after that. And the prayer that He made to the disciples in John Chapter 17, verses 20-26, let us pray that prayer in those six verses, this powerful prayer of reaching out. And my prayer today is there will be an ingathering of souls such as we have never experienced in the history of this church, or any other church. That people will come to Christ. And I believe it will happen. I believe God is working on it even now. I don't know what will trigger it, but I know it's going to happen if we continue to pray, and manifest God's purpose in our Christianity by loving people in the world, as we have been loved by our Savior Jesus Christ. Amen and Amen.

PRAYER WILL KEEP THE DOOR OPEN

Prayer in Persecution

Colossians 4: 2 - 6

This morning we come to the final chapter of the Book of Colossians. This is just such a wonderful book. Paul wrote to the church in Colosse, because there was concern from some of the elders, that the church was letting false religions and philosophies come in and begin to mix with the doctrine of Christianity. Our world is full of it. There's so many different ideologies and philosophies. You can hear about them on television. You go into a truck stop and they've got all these little cassettes, and CD's, and whatever, to tell you how to find this Nirvana, this happiness, this peace. We could go down and name list after list of people who have been searching for something to satisfy the gnawing hunger of their soul. So they're reaching out to these false philosophies. But Paul wanted to emphasize to the Colossians, that Christ is enthroned in heaven. And because of His sacrifice every human being has access to go directly into the presence of God, the holy and righteous God.

God is so holy, that the High Priest under the law, could only go in the Holiest of Holies, where the Ark of the Covenant was, once a year. And if they did anything wrong, because of the righteousness and holiness of God they would be stricken dead. And they had a linen cord that would go outside where the priest would go in, and was tied to his ankle. He had little bells around the lower part of his robe, and if the bell stopped ringing, they would grab the rope and drag the man out. But now we have a new and living way. We come to Christ not on the righteousness of our lives, or our perfection, but on the perfection of Christ in Jesus' name. We can go directly into the presence of the Creator of all things. We now come boldly before God.

Paul talks in Chapter 4 about the mission of the church. Now business goes on, and they talk a lot about their mission statement, what they intend to accomplish. So Paul gives us the mission statement of the church of Jesus Christ. You know what it is? The mission statement of the church, Paul lays it out clearly, is evangelism. It is to bring the good news of the life, death, and resurrection of Jesus Christ, and the fact that every human being has free access into the presence of a holy God. We approach Him not on the basis of our perfection and holiness, but in the name of Jesus Christ. The sacrifice, and the name of Christ completely blot out our transgressions, until God cannot see our weaknesses, our failures, or our sinfulness, because we are covered by the blood, by the sacrifice of Jesus Christ. And you are as holy as any other human being on the face of this earth, when you come to God in and through the name of Jesus Christ. So this is the mission of the church.

The mission of the church includes first of all, prayer. There is nothing spiritually significant that happens without prayer. You say, "What about faith?" Faith comes through hearing the Word of God, and prayer is approaching God, and relating to God. The deeper we get into the Word, and the more we know the Word of God, which is the Word of Christ, the more faith we have. Prayer is the key to heaven. Faith unlocks the door. But the work of evangelism, first of all emphasizes prayer. We pray that we will be able to speak out about Jesus Christ.

Prayer is a part of evangelism. And the reason we should pray, is for God to give us the opportunity to evangelize. We pray for the freedom to speak freely about the Lord Jesus Christ, for God to open the door for our message.

There was a young man stopping off in Greece on a ship, traveling around the world witnessing with Christian young people. He went to the docks and he begun talking to a young person about his salvation, about his relationship with God through Jesus Christ, and he was arrested. It's against the law to bring the message of salvation to anyone in Greece except through the Orthodox Church. You can go to jail for it, and he did go to jail. It took several months for him to get out of jail, simply for talking about Jesus Christ.

We have some persecution in this country. But how many of you know anyone, in this country, who was specifically murdered or arrested because they witnessed to Christ, for Christ? Not really. There's some that have gotten into trouble because they try to do it on the school grounds, or they try to do it in the court house. But the fact is Christians at this point don't suffer greatly for bearing witness to Jesus Christ. And yet as the church is matured, there is less and less witnessing, and there's less and less talking about the message. And so Paul said in the 4th chapter of Colossians, verses 2-4, "Continue earnestly in prayer, being vigilant with thanksgiving, meanwhile praying for us, that God would open a door for the Word, to speak the mystery of Christ, for I am also in chains that I may make it manifest as I ought to speak. So pray, that God will open the door, to my witness and to your witness, to the people around us." That's one of the things that is really missing in the church of Jesus Christ, generally speaking, today. That's why the church is shrinking.

You can say, "Well, there are some huge churches." Yes. But the overall growth of the church simply isn't happening. It's just moving groups of Christians around from different congregations when one church has a more interesting program. They all gather together in larger and larger numbers. And there is more and more pressure to stifle the voice of Christians in our culture. Whether it is through ridicule, through oppression, through ostracization, or rejection, we're very careful not to mention the name of Jesus publicly.

You say "I don't know enough to witness." Did you know that you are the world's leading authority on at least one thing? There is no one in the world that has as much knowledge, and experience, and as much right to speak about one thing. You ask what that is? We can all share our personal testimony of how we came to meet Jesus Christ. You don't have to have a degree from

Fuller Seminary. We can speak right out and say, "I met Christ and He came into my life, and He changed everything, and He gave me joy, and I am so happy about it that I want to share it with everybody."

Now I'm going to tell you something personal. I went fishing Monday, and Tuesday, and Wednesday this last week. And I caught one little fish. But I had my nephew with me and I was teaching him how to fish. Although he knew nothing about how to do it properly, he caught about a nine and a half pound trout; I've not spoken to him since, but I still love him. And he caught a bunch of them. And my friend Jack was with me, and I out fished him; he didn't catch any. I caught one. I caught one that would be bait for Pat's fish.

But the scripture says that we are to be fishers of men. You say, "How do you become a successful fisherman?" You keep fishing. Pat kept standing in the water, it was cold and it was blustery, it was windy, and Jack and I, Raul and my other friend, we kept going into his little trailer house and having coffee. You don't catch many fish from the trailer house. But he was out there, fishing and fishing. I said, "Pat, why didn't you come in and have coffee?" because he caught that nine pounder early. He said, "What if another big one bit while I was having coffee?" You see, that's the kind of zeal that comes into our lives when we first meet Christ. But over the years we've witnessed to all our families. And those that receive Christ, they've received Christ; and the others get ticked off every time you talk about Jesus. So finally we just quit. We're not looking for those opportunities.

He said, "Pray continually, that the door will be open." Pray, there will be freedom to preach the gospel. So when they proclaim the mystery of Christ, for which Paul said, "I am in chains." Paul never backed off. Didn't make any difference what they did him, if they spit on him, they beat him. He said five times "I was beaten with forty stripes save one, a night and a day I was in the deep, I was in chains in prison, I was five times beaten with forty stripes save one." He had that burning zeal, that desire to share the message of Christ. And folks, we have that same calling that God has given us, to talk about the grace of God. And then to pray against evil forces.

Years ago in the Warehouse there was a group, an old rock group named Black Sabbath. They loved to be as blasphemous and as anti-Christian as they possibly could. That's how they made their money. We were having the concerts here and there was a brand new Christian that came up, and he said "Louis, I want you to get up and tell the people to pray the Black Sabbath's concert will fail here at the Memorial Auditorium." I thought, good idea, but without a lot of faith. And so we got up and announced it; we were going to pray against Black Sabbath that their concert wouldn't work. So they came to Sacramento and they started having their well-publicized concert, and their amps blew-up, then they started screaming and cursing at each other. It was in the newspapers the next day. Anyway the concert never happened. And that young man said, "The power of prayer, the power of prayer." You know what? I believe it was the power of prayer.

The power of prayer. God prepares the hearts of people to receive the message. They may not always be ready; you weren't always ready. But the Holy Spirit, when we have a spirit-led led body of believers, will lead us to that person. When the Holy Spirit of God has been working in their life they will open up to the gospel of Jesus Christ.

Think of the powers of evil that would stop us, and then think about the fact that "Greater is He that is in you, than he that is in the world." When you begin to pray and bind the powers of darkness, that devil has no chance at all.

Pray against these false doctrines and vain philosophies that trap the minds of men. Paul states several times in Colossians, he was concerned that believers hang onto sound doctrine, the Word of God, the truth of God. Pray with watchfulness. Paul said one of the reasons we should witness, and one of the reason we should pray, is that we will be ready for the Second Coming of Jesus Christ.

We don't talk about it as much as we did. When the Jesus Movement broke out we were afraid to buy long playing records, because we were afraid we couldn't hear the last song before the Lord came. But the fact of the matter is, Jesus said, "When you begin to hear of wars and rumors of wars, the sea and the waves roaring" and of course that's from Luke and Matthew, and the sea and the wave roaring is the uproar among the human race on planet earth, look up. The turmoil, the uproar, the bloodshed, the violence, the hatred and we're seeing that everywhere, He said "Watch ye therefore, and pray always that you may be accounted worthy to escape these things which are coming to past, and to stand before the son of man." We don't have forever.

Time is precious. Time is the one thing that no matter how rich or how poor you are, you don't have much of when it relates to this earth. Heaven is eternity, there will be no time. But now we are living on the basis of time, and there are things that we should be doing that we don't do, but one of the things God said is, "Watch and pray." It's not just praying for ourselves, but it's praying for others. The scripture talks about the wise and the foolish virgins waiting for the bridegroom to come. Some of them kept oil in their lamps, and kept their lamps refilled; and others got tired of waiting and went to sleep. And when the bridegroom came those whose lamps were not burning were left outside the gates, and those whose lamps were burning went into the gate. They were watching, and some simply got tired of watching and waiting for the bridegroom.

One of the things that I have joy in looking forward to, is the rapture of the church. But I also have sadness. I have grief in my heart when I think about the rapture, because I think about all of the people that I know that don't know Jesus, and I want to share that message with them. There's one thing that I want for all of us, all of you and me, everyone else; I want you to go to heaven and to spend eternity with Jesus Christ. And I want us all to know the truth, and I want it to be based on the scripture, not some kind of promotional physiological babble that is taking place in too many circles of Christianity today. I want you to know there's a heaven to gain, there's a hell to shun. And I want us to understand that, may God pray and give us this desire, and open a door before us, and give us the faith to walk through, that we might personally win somebody to Christ.

I've been praying that God would do something for me, and really help me to touch more lives just as I go about town, go about my life. I have been delivered an edict, and I don't remember where it came from. But every two weeks I have to get a haircut, because I have been praying for these young ladies that cut my hair. So I try to talk to them about the Lord, and ten days ago - I'm four days away from the other one - but I went in and they ask me what I did, and so I started talking about the Lord. There was a young girl that keeps the cash register, and the girl that takes four and a half minutes to cut my hair, so I have to really get with the witnessing. And I talk to her about the Lord, talk to her about church, and Jesus. She said, "You know what, I have never been to church in my life. And I've been thinking lately, I really want to go to church." I said, "You can." And I want to make sure that she cuts my hair for a while. A really wonderful young lady. And then the cash register girl overheard it, she said, "I have never been to church, and no one in my family has ever been to church. But I've been wanting to go."

You see, when you start praying for people, even in the generic sense, God begins to make them conscious of their spiritual need. There is a hunger, and a longing, that only God can place within the spirit, in the soul. And when you're in tune with God, those moments come together.

The Scriptures tells us, the Bible teaches us, "Beloved now we are the children of God, and it does not appear as yet what we will be, but we know that when He appears, we will be like Him because we will see Him just as he is." And everyone who has this hope fixed on Him, purifies himself, just as He is pure; and everyone who practices sin practices lawlessness, and sin in lawlessness. There is a rebellion against God, whether it is subconscious, or conscious inside every human being drifting from the Savior. But the faithful witness of the Holy Spirit is there twenty-four hours a day, seven days a week. But the church needs to awaken again to that driving force, to evangelism.

You say, "But wait a minute. We have these giant meetings." There's a very small percentage of people who come to Christ in those meetings. Billy Graham would tell you himself, and so would Franklyn. He said over 95% of people who come to the crusades didn't come on their own, they were brought by a Christian who had been praying for them. And God used that wonderful ministry to tighten the net and draw them in.

We could go on and talk about a number of things, but the scripture says, that we are not to go around judging the outsiders. You don't win people to Christ by judging them. 1 Corinthians 5:12 and 13 talks about this. The scripture said, "For what have I to do to judge them also that are outside? Do you not judge them that are within? Those who are outside, God judges." The scripture said effectively, you are a spiritual judge of all things; but we judge in our own lives and in the lives of our brothers, and sisters that we might be a warning and an encouragement and strengthening to them. But we have no reason to judge the world. Look at what happens to us.

Jesus set a pattern for witnessing. There was a woman, a Samaritan of mixed race, and as far as Israel was concerned, anyone who was not a Jew was unworthy. They wouldn't even speak to them. But Jesus saw the woman at the well, and He knew her situation. She'd been married seven times, and she probably had all sorts of immorality in her life. But Jesus goes up to her and said, "Would you get me some water?" Because He saw the desperate thirst in her life. He didn't just focus in and say, "You got to change your way of living, you know, you got to quit marrying men for a hobby, you got to do something else with your life. You know this is terrible, this is a reproach to the culture." The world saw her as that woman that's been married over, and over again; and now that she is getting older, she cannot find anybody to marry her anymore. Jesus saw a human being. He didn't see a statistic, He didn't see just a number, He saw a hungering, longing spirit that was in desperate need of knowing God. And He says "Listen, the water that I give you will satisfy your thirst and you will never thirst again."

What about the woman caught in adultery? She was an object of ridicule and scorn, and according to the law she should be stoned. Have you ever thought of the fact? Here she is, this woman was in the act of adultery, so there was a man with her. But the man got off fine. You see in our culture, and in the world's culture, men could get by with sowing their wild oats. God doesn't look at it that way. So they brought just the woman to Jesus.

So Jesus what does he do? He doesn't look at the woman and scorn her. They say, "What did the law say you need to do to her? The law said we need to stone her." So, they expected Jesus to say, "Let's go get some rocks and take care of this woman." No, he just stooped down on the ground, and he begins to write. And one of the guys standing there looked down, "I know where you were two nights ago," and the man slunk away. He started writing stuff about all these people. Pretty soon there was nobody left. Jesus said to her, "Where are your accusers?" And He forgave her, He said, "Go and sin no more." That's all he said. Because sin is hurting you, sin is crushing your life, sin is leaving you empty. And I have something to give you that will satisfy you, I have something that is wonderful.

When we talk to people about the Lord, we should speak to them in grace. It's what the scripture talks about. To evangelize is to speak in grace and saltiness. What does salt do? Salt heals and preserves. If you can't find any Neosporin or anything like that, and you've got a cut or a wound, pack it with salt. It's a little memorable when you do it, but the fact is it will purify and preserve that wound. It really will. So we speak to people in grace - with graciousness. Grace means unmerited favor of God. We don't care what they do or what they were, a prostitute or a tax collector they are favored by God for forgiveness. This is what Jesus did, He talked with tax collectors, the prostitute, the rich young ruler, every class of society, because Jesus didn't see anybody in that manner. Shortly before His crucifixion, a woman came in with a broken heart, with tears streaming down her face, and everyone knew she was a woman of low moral reputation. She poured this expensive oil on His feet. They looked at Jesus and said, "He must not be God or He wouldn't let such a person be around Him." And she washed His feet with her tears, and bathed them in ointment and dried them with her hair. And Jesus read their minds, and said, "She is the only one here that knows what's really happening. She's come to anoint my body for the burying." And Mary Magdalene stood with Him at the cross.

We close by looking again at Colossians 3:12, "Therefore as the elect of God, holy and beloved," I love this verse, "put on tender mercies, kindness, humility, meekness, forgiving one and other. If anyone have a complaint against another, even as Christ forgave you, so also must you do. But above all these things put on love, which is the bond of perfection."

Help us Lord to see people as you see them. Not as the world sees them, not as the culture sees them, for you look upon our hearts. And as we live in prayer and walk in the spirit, give us a capacity to understand what's going on in other's lives. Help us to show you're not condemning us, but we're all sinners saved by grace.

THREE PHASES OF PRAYER
Supplication, Intercession, Thanksgiving
1 Timothy 2:1-8

This morning we're going to turn to Chapter 2 of 1st Timothy and share the first two verses. This is Paul's second assignment to Timothy. His first assignment was to go to the church at Ephesus and correct doctrinal errors, to discipline some who had strayed from the faith, and bring the church in line with the revealed Word of God. And you recall when Paul last met with the elders from Ephesus, there on the island by the seashore, he looked at them and he said, "I really don't know if I will ever see you again."But he said, "It breaks my heart."That's what he was saying; some of you who are standing here now in harmony with God, in fellowship with God, trusting in the Word, will turn away; become opponents of the truth of the gospel. So he sent this young man, in his early to mid-twenties, to correct a church that was one of the older churches at that time in the New Testament.

He shares with Timothy some things that he wanted to stress. The need for obedience to God, and the need to turn away from false doctrines. There were some in the church that were teaching that the resurrection had already come. There was a lot of grief in the church because many thought that they had missed out, and would now enter into the tribulation period. They totally misconstrued the scripture. And so Timothy had that unenviable job of coming in and bringing correction to the church in these controversial areas that were destructive to the faith.

Paul said, "Therefore I exhort first of all," it's kind of a nice way to say, "I command you." It's not a good thing, this is not a pattern for your marriage relationship, to say "I command you," it's not really a good approach. So I think "exhort" will also be a word you will leave out of your communication with each other. "Therefore I exhort first of all, that supplications, prayers, intercessions, and giving thanks be made for all men. For kings and all who are in authority, that we may lead a quiet and peaceable life in all godliness and reverence."

So the apostle is talking about three phases of prayer. Actually, there is a slightly different word in the Greek that you find with most of the references to prayer. It talks about a universal prayer for the needs of humanity, through the church of Jesus Christ. Then he also mentions the supplications and so forth, and intercessions that God would have us do.

Let's pray. Lord we stand at a time, when our world and our nation is in a precarious predicament. There are more and more nations that are rising up with weapons that would destroy masses of humanity, in a moment's time. Lord, you know the problems that we face in the world. We look at it sometimes and our hearts tremble, as we see governments that had walked with you, turn away from you and seek to implement the very things that you command us to abstain from in the Word of God. But you are in control. And we pray, Lord, for the governments, we pray for our nation, our city, the area that we live in. We pray for the world that you placed us in, that Jesus might reveal himself to masses of people. Lord, we pray for you to come and divinely intervene in the affairs of men, and draw men's heart to your lovely son Jesus. Speak to our heart this morning, as we present this word, we ask this in Jesus' name. Amen.

One writer put it very well, when he talked about prayer in the sense that we pray together in a church service. He said that when we come together in a church service and we pray, that it is the people of God encountering God himself, on behalf of their fellow Christians and people in the world around. This is what public prayer is for. We gather together, we pray together, we join together, join our hearts. And when we pray, we begin to pray about the things that are the great concerns in the heart of our heavenly Father. God doesn't want one human being, whoever he was, is, or will be, to be lost for all eternity. And we will talk about that later in these eight verses of 1 Timothy Chapter 2.

This is the emphasis of our services. To come together and let our minds move away from the challenges, and the things of life for a while. To focus our attention instead on the greatness, and the love, and the power of the God that we serve. We all have problems, because if nobody is a problem we make ourselves a problem."We flee when no man pursueth," that's what the Bible says. There is this element of prayer that the Bible talks about. We begin to see the magnificence, the power of God, the greatness of God. And when we come together in corporate worship, and we pray, and we sing praises to God, something mysterious and wonderful often happens; the problems that seems so big, and insurmountable, and so threatening, diminish.

I didn't ask permission, but I'm going to take a chance on saying something publicly. I was at our Tuesday night Christianity Explored meeting. And when I got home, I was pretty late, but I got a little message from Bill and Jeanie. Bill's been going through some real challenges, suddenly his blood had turned bad, in his terms, cancerous. And he was in and out hospital for all kinds transfusions, he was given little to no hope. And when I listen to that voice mail, I heard such joy, such faith. He said, "I had to share this with you." And I'm going to mess it up, but you can talk to him afterwards and get the real version. He said, "I saw the doctor yesterday." This is the same doctor that didn't give any hope. I mean they are wonderful people, I am an admirer of people in the medical profession, whether they have any faith or not. God gives them that knowledge, and that is a part of His healing to the nations, and to the people of the world. But the ultimate healing always comes from God. So there's this cancerous blood disease, without a lot of hope, Bill was gearing himself up for another round of chemo. Some of you've been through that, you know how fun that is. And he said, "I am only going to go through one more treatment," and then the doctor said, "Things are looking really good." And she said, "We're just going to keep tabs on you, see you every once in a while into the future. The bad cells, the cancer cells are diminishing, and I think you are going to be fine."

But what a wonderful thing that God did, and this comes about because of prayer. I'm praying for a number of people going through similar circumstances. I'm praying for people whose marriages are on the verge of collapse, who have bitterness towards each other in their homes. I'm praying for people who have been out of work, some of them over a year, and they're looking for employment. I'm praying for all kinds of things. And if I had to stand there and say, "Oh Louis, what are you going to do about it?" I would be totally discouraged. But I'm not, because nothing is too hard for the Lord. Prayer is what changes things. You ever hear that term, "prayer changes things?" It does. It changes them for the good, for the glory of God. Problems are solved with corporate worship and prayers.

I was looking at Psalm 73, and David was going through a really terrible time. His enemies were beating up on him, and it seemed as though everything was dark. David could get into a major blue funk, you just read some of his writings. That's a theological term. And he was just talking about how good the wicked were doing, and he was doing badly, and how he was being persecuted, abused, lied about, cheated on.... you can go on and on. Read it in Psalm 73. And you know what he said? He said something that's kind of interesting in 73:17 Psalm; "..until I went in to the sanctuary of God, then I understood." That's why God wants you to go to church. Because your focus is on the greatness of God, not the malignant, malevolent problems that hover over our consciousness and our subconscious minds. Problems are solved when we come into the presence of God.

One of the forms of prayer is supplications. When we submit a supplication, it is a prayer request that is bringing someone else's need before the throne of God. We bring a request for someone else, in supplication to God, or some need in supplication to God. And the scripture tells us to do this. Galatians 6 and 2 says, "Bear one another's burdens, and so fulfill the law of Christ." Listen to people that have challenges and problems in their life, and pray for them, and God will speak to you.

This is one of the things that God wants us to do; come before Him with supplications. I am coming for supplications for people that are sick, people that are needy, and most of all for people who don't know the Lord. People who don't know Jesus, that's the greatest focus of my prayer. Spiritual sickness and death is the greatest sickness that exist, and it is one that never ends for all eternity, unless it is healed by the saving grace of Jesus Christ. Supplications bring that person's name specifically before the Lord. That's what this prayer in the Bible is talking about.

Then there's intercession. It's like an intimate petition made by a friend to a king on behalf of somebody. "Lord, I bring so and so before you." There are young people I know who were raised in this church, they're not walking with the Lord. And many times the Holy Spirit lays them on my heart, and I bring their name specifically before the throne of grace. And if you have a child or a loved one who used to walk with the Lord, and now has turned away from the Lord, give me the privilege of slipping it in an envelope, and putting it in one of the offering things or give it to somebody at the desk. I want those names because I want to pray for all of them. I pray for as many as I know about, but I want to pray for all of them, because I want to make intersession on behalf of the needs of these people, and bring them back to Christ.

I know of scores and scores of people who strayed, got pretty beat up, and now they are back serving the Lord, and strong in the faith because we don't give up on them. We keep praying, we keep seeking God, and the power of heaven comes to bear on their lives. And sooner or later they will be forced to make a decision whether they want to come back to God, or continue in their rebellion against God. And if that's their choice, then there's nothing we can do about that, because God will not force Himself on any one. Prayer focuses our hearts and our eyes upon God, as we acknowledge His power.

Then there's thanksgiving. This is one of the reasons that I really encourage everybody to be on time. Because what happens when we sing our choruses? Most of the choruses are "Oh I thank you Lord, yes I thank you Lord, for all the things you've done and who you are." Those choruses cycle through my mind every day. And I sing those songs of praise and worship, and thanksgiving, because He said also to praise with thanksgiving. So I urge people to sing, to worship, to give praise to God. One of the things you can do is to drive down the highway and sing choruses to God, sing hymns to God. The scriptures says, "Singing psalms and hymns in your heart, singing and making melody unto the Lord." Giving praise to God, giving thanks to God. You say, "Well, there are so many things I don't have." But you got a lot of things that you should thank God for, because the others are on the way, if they were this good for you, if it's the will of God for you.

Who should we pray for? Well this is the tough one. For all people. When it talks about "for all men" it's speaking in its generic term, a biblical term, in this particular phrase, men and women. We're to pray for all people, all human beings. Pray for kings and all in position of authority, all without distinction. I want you to think about this. You may not be happy with whatever government we have. I don't know. But Paul wrote those words when Nero, one of the most vicious Emperors who ever lived ruled. Full of the Devil, he took Christians and impaled them on stakes while they were alive, covered them with oil and lit them, and used them as light for his drunken orgies and parties. And Paul said "Pray for him, pray for him." Wouldn't it be really cool if all the Democrats prayed for the Republicans and the Republicans all prayed for the Democrats. Wouldn't that be cool? If they really meant it, it could change things.

The scripture said that prayer can affect a country. Now I am deeply concerned about what's going on in our country. I'm concerned about the new morality that is being preached, from the universities, from the government, from the entertainment industry, and so on. God is the better way for us to live, a better plan. So you say, "Well, how can I pray then for a president, for a Congress, that believes it's a good thing to have abortion, that it's a good thing to have same sex marriages, it's a good thing to have people live outside of wedlock until more than 50 percent of our children are born without both parents in the home?"

A single mother goes through tremendous suffering, need, and poverty, because she's forsaken and left alone to raise children. And I tell you something; I admire single mothers and single fathers who love their children so much, that they will give themselves and live a very sacrificial life to see their children make it through. As a church we want you to know, we love you, and we support you and we want to help every way we can with your children. But God's best is for men and women, a husband and a wife, to raise children together, that's what God desires. So I pray for that. I pray children will have mothers and fathers who love them. The only way that's going to happen on a large scale, is if we really turn to Jesus for His help and His strength.

So we pray. You say, "What difference does it make?" If you disagree biblically, theologically with the direction the government is going, then we are to pray? Proverbs 21:1 says, "The king's heart is in the hands of the Lord like the rivers of water, he turns it whatever way he wishes." God can actually change the mind of a leader away from darkness to something that is upright and righteous, if we pray for them. We have to pray for them. And I've really failed in this area. As I've studied this out, I've prayed more this week for our President than I ever have. I haven't really prayed that much for presidents and people in authority, and people in leadership, yet it's a direct commandment of God. And we need to do that, that's a part of our prayer life.

When we pray things happen; first within us, and then outside of us. When we begin to pray things change, we suddenly look up and say, "That seemed pretty impossible; but now it just seems like a minor irritant." It's because you're not alone, the power of God is there. So we'll talk a little bit more about this.

Now 1 Timothy 2: 3-7. I want to read them this morning. "For this is good and acceptable in the sight of God our Savior; who will have all men to be saved, and to come unto the knowledge of the truth. For there is one God, and one mediator between God and men, the man Christ Jesus, who gave himself a ransom for all, to be testified in due time. Whereunto I am ordained a preacher, and an apostle, (I speak the truth in Christ, and lie not;) a teacher of the Gentiles in faith and verity." So what is God saying here? He's saying, "I want every human being to be saved." Now I know people have a different theological vision of God, that we are all predestined and predetermined and we have nothing to do with it. I don't believe that. The Bible says right here, and He says it in many places, that "I want all men to be saved." That is the desire. That is the purpose of God in creating you. That is what God wants in our lives.

The scripture says in 2 Peter 3:9, "The Lord is not slack concerning His promise, as some men count slackness; but is longsuffering to us-ward, not willing that any should perish, but that all should come to repentance." And the Bible says, "For God so loves the world, He gave His only begotten son; that whosoever believes in Him, shall not perish but have everlasting life. For God sent not His son into the world to condemn the world, but that the world through Him might be saved."

So I know from the scripture God wants every human being, every soul, every spirit of man to be saved, to turn from darkness to light. Jesus said it. But I also know He said in Matthew 7:14, "Narrow is the gate, and difficult is the way which leads to life, and there are few that finds it. But broad and smooth and easy is the path that leads to perdition." God will not condemn us. Somebody said, "But why would God send people to an everlasting hell?" In the truer sense he doesn't. There's one door that leads to safety. There's one door that satisfies the justice of God, and that is the person of Jesus Christ. I have somebody say to me, "You are so bigoted and narrow, saying that Jesus is the only way to God," and I said "I didn't say it, He did. I repeated it, and I believe it." And then I was able to share why I believe that. And he said, "You're still a bigot". Anyway, we had a nice talk.

Trusting in God's meritorious death alone, we're to pray without wrath, having no vindictive feeling towards others as we go to prayer. We're not to harbor an unforgiving spirit as we go to prayer. And if someone offends us we forgive them, even if they don't ask forgiveness. We forgive because we've been forgiven. The scriptures says, "Lifting holy hands, and giving praise to God without wrath and doubting." It was a custom among the Jewish worshipers that they would wash their hands symbolically, a way of saying that "I've been cleansed from living for the world, I'm living now for God. I want to present clean hands before him. I don't want any hatred, any animosity, any bitterness in my heart when I come before God." I want to come with clean hands and lift up my hands to God and begin to worship him. Come relying on the promises of God, and the sacrifice and mediation of Jesus, putting away all sin and living a holy life without doubting. This is what God wants. I would that man everywhere will lift holy hands giving praise to God.

When they would bring an animal sacrifice, and the sins of the man would temporarily be placed on that animal sacrifice, to show the wages of sin is death, they would lift up their hands and put their hands on the animal sacrifice. And then the animal's life would be taken to show how devastating and terrible that sin was. Sin brings death. Then you find in the scripture where when God sets people free, they would lift up their hands in prayer, and praise and thanksgiving.

Isn't that interesting, that when somebody puts a gun in your face, the first thing you what to do is lift your hands? We don't lift our hands because God has a gun on our face, we lift our hands because we're reaching out to a Father that loves us, like a little kid. Ah man, remember those days, remember those days when you had a little child that was yours, they'd come running across the park, "I'm coming daddy, I'm coming." "Oh wow, what do you want kid, I'll give you anything you want, just come hug me." "I'm coming Daddy. I'm coming Daddy. I want to see you Daddy."

I see people, when they've been gone on military duty for so long, when they come home - I'm not much for tears - but those public service announcements where they show these soldiers, men and women coming home to their families, and their kids look up and see them, and they run and grab them. Man, that's

Kleenex time for me. And we have a Father that feels that way about us. I might be big and ugly but I'm coming Daddy, because we're beautiful in His sight. Every one of us. And that's the power of prayer, the power of intercession, bringing someone's need before God. Being received with open arms by a loving Father, who placed all of our sins upon His only begotten son.

I've talked it about so often, as Easter comes this is on my mind frequently. I cannot understand that mysterious thing, that in the darkness of the cross, the pure and Holy Jesus, experienced the transference of all of the sins of the whole human race; past, present, and future. A shift from the sins of men to His sinless human body. What a crushing load. And His righteousness went to us, and covered us. Scripture says, "He became sin, that we might be redeemed." And it is by that sacrifice we come into the presence of God. Don't ever give up on anybody, because the Bible said, "God is not willing that any perish, but that all come to repentance." We're always hearing things in our sports culture, you know, let's take it up a notch. Well, could I encourage you to take your prayer life up a notch, and see what God will do.

I wasn't going to share this, but I just feel like it's important, so I'm going to do it. I saw a person the other day in a grocery store that has been through some terrible trials. Death, loss, health, having very little working at a very low paying job. We were in a public place but I said, "Well can I pray with you" and we prayed together for a minute. It was just quiet - nothing like, "Oh God!" Just a quiet prayer. I walked away, and God spoke to my heart. It was so clear. He said, "I want you to give that person $200." And I said, "Oh Lord, I have to go to the bank." I didn't hear Him say it, but I know that He was sending me to the bank. And I came back and just shook hands and left it there. Now I don't know if I'm going to lose my reward in heaven or not, but I know one thing, I walked away feeling richer than before I did, because I was used of God. And we can do it with a kind word; see somebody that have a need, you have the power to meet that need. Then that's a part of prayer.

There are things that God shows us in prayer we can do, there are other things only God can do. And that's why we need to have all kinds of prayer. Somebody has an obvious need, "Oh I could help with that. I could do that." And then there's things only God can do. Only God can heal a broken heart, only God can bring peace and hope when we've lost a love one, only God can heal our bodies. It goes on and on. But there's something we can all do, and that's what Jesus wants us to do. He said "I want you to go out and do the work that I was doing when I was here, because I want to do it through you." The only way we will do that, is to stay in tune in prayer.

So let me encourage you. Don't get in your rut; jump up in the morning, hopefully brush your teeth and get on with life, but take a little time to meditate in prayer. Say "God, what would you have me do today?" And He will bless you, and lift your spirits, and take the focus off of your problems, and put your mind on the glory of God and the privilege it is to be a representative and ambassador of the King.

PRAY NOT TO BE RICH

Materialism or Spirituality
1 Timothy 6:4-19

What about wealth, as a Christian? What should be our attitude be? What place should wealth, material wealth, play in our lives? The apostle Paul deals with this in many places in scripture, but he also lays it out very clearly in the Book of 1st Timothy Chapter 6, verses 4 through 8. He tells us what God's purpose is for wealth, and how it should affect our lives.

Father, thank you for the Word, and we pray you will speak to our hearts and give us peace and direction as we listen to your Word. And may the Holy Spirit help us to apply it to our lives, and be free from the snares that come through this desire, a longing that is constantly paraded before us in our culture, to obtain wealth, and to have everything that we want materially. We pray that you'll bless us, you'll draw us closer to Jesus, and show us the source of true wealth today. We ask this in Jesus' name, Amen.

I don't know if you've ever experienced this but somebody wins a big jackpot in the lottery and you think, "Wow, wish that was me." You know, "It should have been me, I deserve it they don't. I don't even know them but they don't deserve it as much as I do." And so you get those thoughts going in your mind that this would really make you happy. We're coming to football season and you hear these contracts, these great contracts that some of these football players get. You say, "Wow. You know, they got a $100 million." Well they really didn't, the government got $50 million, their representation got 10 %, and some of them their first, second or third ex-wives get another percent, and they don't end up with very much, relatively speaking. But the fact is, it is still a lot of money. You see it in the theater, the actors so forth, and so on. But you look at that and you realize that in the lottery, 70% of the people who win the lottery are broke in just a few years. 78% of the professional football players that get these great contracts are broke within a few years. And there is not the satisfaction and fulfillment they believe is available in great wealth.

There was a person who sang in a choir in England many years ago, many, many years ago because this person is now very, very old. He was a great athlete, sang in the church choir. He had an accident where he was playing soccer or some game, and he stumbled and ended up biting off the tip of his tongue. This changed the way he spoke. So he became a rock musician. And he wrote a song that tells us how he ended up, he said, "I just can't get no satisfaction and I've tried and I've tried and I've tried;" that's Mick Jagger. He became famous because he sacrificed the piece of his tongue so he could talk funny. But there is no satisfaction. I don't know anything about his personal spiritual life, nor him personally. But I do know that at one time he heard a little scripture, because he was in the church choir, he probably sang Christian songs. At one time he was involved in an entirely different lifestyle. Now he has attained everything that multitudes of young people wish to attain; fame, fortune, hedonistic lifestyle, having everything you want when you want it, and still he sings one of the most popular rock songs of all times about having no satisfaction.

And that's the way of the world. First Timothy Chapter 6, verses 6 through 8 says, "Now godliness with contentment is great gain. For we brought nothing into the world and it is certain we can carry nothing out. And having food and clothing, with these things we shall be content." What is the key, what is the secret to peace, contentment and satisfaction? The scripture lays it out very, very plainly. Twice in these verses Paul points out that the scripture teaches us that great wealth is really contentment in God. That's where great wealth is, that's where satisfaction is. Satisfaction of course is a synonym for contentment. We can also talk about gratification, fulfillment, happiness. But Paul tells us that true contentment is not a matter of material wealth, or physical well-being alone, it is a relationship with God. It is an understanding of exactly who we really are, and what it takes to bring fullness of soul, and spirit, and peace within the inner man. Confidence not only in life, but in death, and out into eternity.

Contentment as a Christian comes from a whole and a balanced life. We are body, soul and spirit. We cannot satisfy the needs of the spirit, no matter what we attain through our body or through our soul - which is our intellect. We simply cannot find fulfillment. And the world testifies to that every single day of our lives. Wholeness, richness of soul and spirit. "Godliness is great gain," He said. And the fruit of a life that is void of God is a tragedy, because there is a longing within us for more than just the physical realm, we are a spiritual creation. Some people think, "Well if I could just have this person, marry this person or that person in my life …. I don't need God. I just need that person." But there are millions and millions of people that found that didn't work out so well. You just wake up one morning and, "Oh thank God she is there and thank God he is here," and then years later you say, "Oh my God, she is still here," or "Oh my God he is still there."

That's because we put the physical, the mental and the emotions above the spiritual. Unless we are spiritually fulfilled, we cannot find satisfaction and contentment anywhere else. But if you have spiritual fellowship with God, and a relationship with God, you can have peace, and you can have fulfillment in any particular pattern of life.

We are so wrapped up in our culture and materialism, blatant hedonism. I was listening to a conversation in a booth behind us at a Chinese restaurant some time back. And it became so offensive that I felt like getting up in the middle of that restaurant and preaching a sermon to these four young jerks, I mean these four young men sitting behind me. I really did. I thought, what empty, shallow, vicious people they really are. They were talking about a young woman that all four of them had had sexual relationships with. They were mocking her, they were making fun of her. They were ridiculing her body, her mind, her soul. They cared nothing for her, and yet they wanted to use her for gratification of their sexual desires. They had absolutely no tenderness, no humanity, no real love, no real care, they were totally wrapped up in fulfilling their own desires. And they used her - had this woman heard those words her life would be crushed. And it will be anyway, unless she finds fulfillment that comes from God. And the same is true of them.

This is a part of our culture though; we are a rootless, restless people in this country. We are constantly looking for something in our lives to deaden the pain. There is a lot of pain in our lives. There is a lot of pain when somebody rejects us, somebody mocks us, and somebody takes the most precious things that we have and absolutely spits upon them and defiles them. There is a pain that comes in our lives when you overhear somebody saying some terrible thing, and they don't have any idea how badly you are hurting.

Well, we have been paying quite a price. 30% of Americans abuse alcohol. Some are just trying to get rid of the pain, some trying to find some happiness, some fulfillment, and others don't know. The scripture said, "Where your treasure is there will your heart be also." Americans spent over $13.1 billion on pornography last year. All it does is create unrealistic expectation, and robs the sanctity, and the purity, and the beauty of married life, the intimacy God intended between a man and a woman. Did you know that one third of all pornography is watched by women? It's kind of sad when we are dragging women down to our level. It's really sad. They are the child bearers, they are the care givers; it is the coarsening of our culture.

And what is it doing for you? It's not easing the pain. That doesn't even talk about all the prescription drugs to try to help us get along in life. But we look at all of these things to try to ease the pain. We keep looking for help in all the wrong places, looking for fulfillment in a place where it does not exist. And turning our back on the one source of fulfillment - which is an intimate, loving, caring relationship with a loving God He loves us so much that He poured His life upon that cross, and took the humiliation and shame of our sins upon Himself, and gave us a new life that will bring life into a bright color and fulfillment. This is what God desires of us. But the Bible tells us, "Where your treasure is there will your heart be also." And look at the places we spend our time and spend our money; on material things, on mental things that are sometimes extremely unhealthy. On striving for positions, striving to be acknowledged, striving somehow to be fulfilled. We spend it in the wrong place, but we only have so much to spend. We have whatever money God entrusts to us. And more precious still; we only have so much time. I don't want to depress you but I recognized, this is a profound thought, I am closer to the end of the popsicle than I was when I started. You can put that on your refrigerator, it will be a comfort.

Some think of contentment as getting anything they want, whenever they want it. I was up at Pyramid lake fishing with a friend of mine a few months ago, and there was this old gentlemen. He was a character. Some people were offended by him, because he was 84 years old and he is still out there fishing. He is short, and he has a little ladder that he stands on to fish, and he has his bucket in front of him where he takes the sinking line and pulls it. And he makes this great cast. Next to him was a guy asking him how he was catching all those fish. I kind of kept track of him that day and talked to him later; he caught fifty seven trout from three pounds up to twelve and a half pounds that day; and released them. And here was this guy, he'd been to Cabela's, which is a sporting goods store. He'd spent $900 on a fly rod that is the best in the business. He'd spent - the whole total bill, and he happened to mention this in a whole profane way, "I spent blankety blank on this and this guy over here has caught all this fish and I haven't caught one." He had all of this fancy equipment, everything. But he couldn't cast the line out of his shadow. I don't know what he expected; for the fish to say, "We'll help you? We'll come in really close to you and bite for you because you spend all this money and you obviously look like a great fishermen ought to look on television...." But here he was, he had all of this stuff and he slammed his rod down. I thought, "If you don't want it..." No satisfaction, no satisfaction.

You look at all the different little things that we go through trying to find fulfillment, trying to find satisfaction when it's not available, except through Jesus Christ. Because as long as you don't have Him, your restless, troubled, soul will be searching for something to take His place. And there is no human being that can take His place. There is no amount of money, there is no amount of prestige, there is no amount of power. There is no amount of anything that can fill the place that He alone can fill; because that's how we were built. That's how God made us! He placed within us this object, this emptiness, that can only be filled by Jesus.

In the Book of Philippians, Paul talks about the secret in the 4th chapter. He said, "I am not talking about any personal need that I might have, but I have learnt in whatever state I am to be content." Paul said, my happiness does not depend upon my circumstances. And this is a man that was in prison, that was beaten, that was shipwrecked, that went through terrible suffering for the cause of Christ. And he goes on to tell us, "I know how to be abased." In other words, I know how to do without and still have contentment. He said, and this is important, "I know how to abound." I know how to be in prosperous times, when all of my physical and material needs are met. I am able to handle that too. But he went on to say, "Everywhere and in all things, I have learnt both to be full and to be hungry, both to abound and to suffer need. I can do all things through Christ who strengthens me." He said, my contentment is not held hostage to my circumstances. There is a definition of true godliness that we are putting up on the screen now and you'll have to think about it a little bit; at least I did. The definition of true godliness is, "When you have God and food and clothing and shelter; that is all you really need to be enriched, and fulfilled, and satisfied, and content."

Luke Chapter 2, verse 15. "And He said to them, 'Take heed, beware of covetousness. For one's life does not consist in the abundance of the things he possesses.'" Paul proves this by his example that follows up here. He begins to liken it to life and death. I was with a dear friend who was going through a time of great struggle, and finally he went to be with the Lord. And I saw he was very troubled at one time, and I looked over at him and I said, "Are you concerned about the business, because someone had been talking about business." And he said, "At this point I don't care about the business. At this point I don't care." Why? Because he was ready to go to heaven, and all of these things that he had were left behind him.

Someone said the other day, it was written that this man died a multi-billionaire. That's not true. When you die you don't have anything. Everything you have goes to someone else, but when you're dead you don't have anything. You might be like that guy who was buried in his '56 Cadillac convertible in Texas, because he just loved that car and he is literally buried in it. It's on a highway and there is a little sign there between Austin and San Antonio Texas. He is buried in his Cadillac. He is sitting behind the wheel to this day. But I got news for him and for you; he is sitting there but he isn't going anywhere. There is too much dirt around him to drive, and there is nothing in his body that even cares. His soul and spirit have departed into eternity. I hope his real value was in Christ. If not, the Bible said, it would be better for him had he never been born. This is simply the truth, this is what the scripture says.

Job said it really well. He said, "Naked I came from my mother's womb and naked I return, back to the earth from which I came." So we die no matter how they dress us up. I don't know why we put our best suit on when we die but that's kind of a tradition, that's alright. Whatever we can do to bring comfort and help to the families, I'm not criticizing it, I am not taking it lightly, whatever comforts. But the minute that soul is gone, dies, when you die your spirit and your soul is gone.

For those who desire to be rich, 1st Timothy 6 verse 9 says, "Fall into temptation and snare and to many foolish harmful lusts which drown men into destruction and perdition." How many times have you thought you wanted something, you saved for it, you looked for it, and suddenly you had it? And that happened to me just recently. I have a boat that's kind of an antique, I have had it so long. I keep it at a friend's house up in the mountains.

I wanted a depth finder, and a fish finder, so I didn't have to work so hard finding the fish. If you know how to work it, it shows the fish as little skeletons and I was so excited about that. So I had my brother with me, and we took our little annual three day trip; we took it out and I was all excited, we were going to use it. We couldn't turn it on, and when we did it didn't work. I mean it does all of these things, but I can't figure it out. I watched the video, I studied three books, I have no idea how to use it. It's supposed to tell you where you've been, where you're going, whether heaven or hell - no it doesn't do that, but it tells you where you've been or where you going all this kind of stuff. It plots the course, shows you where the little fishes are, the big fishes; and it's all in the video. But it didn't do me any good. A friend of mine used the boat and called me up last Thursday and he said, "Louis", he said, "I was so excited to go out and use that new fish finder. I studied the material you left me." And he said, "I got it on but all it would do is give me is the name of the product; and that's all it would do, and then I couldn't turn it off. So," he said, "I had to unscrew it, I hope it didn't damage it." And in my heart I said I hope it did. That thing deserves to die. But that's kind of the way material things are.

Paul talks about temptations being a snare. "If I could just have this, do that, do something else." So the scripture goes on and really warns us, in 1st Timothy 6:9; "But those who desire to be rich fall into temptation and snare and into many foolish and harmful lusts which drown men in destruction and perdition." Wealth gives us access to more things that can destroy us. The attainment never matches up to the pursuit. The scripture goes on and said, "We become a prey to senseless, and harmful desires." We do. You know something interesting, if you're really, really wealthy, I've seen many, many guys in the Hawaiian Islands that are like in their sixties, and seventies, and ninety fives, and what have you. But anyway it's an amazing thing. I am thinking they're out having a wonderful time with their daughter and I find out it's their wife. And I look at his wrinkled, poor old body, and all of the sags, tucks and wrinkles, and all of the plastic surgeries until he can't even smile. He's wearing young, young clothes as though we'll look at him and say, "Oh, he is young, he's got young clothes. Wow, look at that." The trouble of it is, those young clothes weren't made for bulges and sags. And I thought, "Here he is, and he has her, she is a part of his possessions. And why was she attracted to him? Because of his great personality, because of his intellect, she just thought he was the coolest thing ever?" And you wonder why she is winking at the busboy.

And so we look at these things, and we think we want them, and we desire them, and sometimes they simply just don't work out. Because there is no contentment, there is no fulfillment, there is no satisfaction outside of Jesus. It's the only place you'll find it. But remember this; the Bible didn't say money was evil. The Bible said, the love of money is evil. You don't have to be rich to love money. There was a guy way back in the past times when he walked up to a very wealthy industrialist there in New York City. And he had a beautiful suit on you know, with the vest, he had the gold watch chain on, and not only did he have a gold watch chain going across his chest, but he had a little fob that was full of diamonds. The man went up and he said, "You are so proud of that chain and that watch and your wealth." The industrialist looked at him, and he had some baling twine hooked across his old torn up and battered shirt and inside his pocket was his watch. And he said, "I perceive sir that you have more pride in your possessions than I have in mine, because they mean nothing to me now. They did but not now, not now."

So the scripture says, "For the love of money is the root of all kinds of evil, from which some have strayed from the faith and pierced themselves through with many sorrows." The love of money, not money itself. There is a quote. Here's what destination sickness is. "It's arriving at your destination, being where you always wanted to be, having everything you always wanted to have, but not wanting anything you've got." And how many people do you know does that happen to?

The abundance of a man's life does not consist of the things he possesses. Is the Bible against wealth? No, absolutely not. But skipping down to the 17th verse, Paul lays out the pattern that God has set for us, as He prospers us and blesses us. "Command those who are rich in this present age not to be haughty, nor to trust in uncertain riches but in the living God who gives us richly all things to enjoy." That's what the scripture says. If you are blessed, and you are rich in the present world, don't trust in those riches, because they will fail you. And as Job said, naked you came into this world, naked you go out, you take nothing with you. Absolutely nothing, materially or physically. Nor do you keep anything on this earth that is spiritual or mental; because of those elements of mankind, body, soul and spirit, the soul and the spirit flee, either up to the presence of God or down into the place of eternal regrets and pain.

The scripture also says, don't be haughty. Don't credit yourself with financial success. If you were born in the slums of Calcutta, India or other places in the world, you wouldn't be where you are today. When you look around in most of the world, even the poorest among us is richer than most in this world. Being rich does not change who you are, it doesn't make any difference, and Jesus talks about the deceitfulness of riches. He says "Now, he who receives the seeds among the thorn is he who hears the Word and the cares of this world, and the deceitfulness of riches chokes the Word and then becomes unfruitful."

I don't know how many people I've known over the years especially, as a young man in Texas, where wealth would suddenly come quickly through energy, through oil, through gas and through other natural products; and then suddenly these people would have all of this wealth. Now all of a sudden, they had no time for God, church, or service. 1st Timothy Chapter 6 verses 18 and 19 said, "Let them do good that they be rich in good works, ready to give, willing to share, storing up for themselves a good foundation for the time to come that they may hold of eternal life." So the scripture says, use your money in ways that help people build the kingdom of God; pour it out don't waste it, it's a valuable commodity.

You don't have to love money to have money, sometimes God gives you a gift an opportunity and ability. He gives you the strength of mind to take advantage of it, and the wealth begins to accumulate, and then you have a greater responsibility than you had when you were poor. To whom much is given, much is required. And God said when you prosper it's not just for you to have time to play your way into eternity. Also be rich in good deeds. Don't only just give money, but be personally involved in serving God, and serving people with your time. Be liberal and generous, that's what the scripture says, be liberal and generous. Jesus went on to say "Freely you've received, freely give."

Everything we have comes from God, every opportunity. We sing that song; "Great is thy faithfulness, all I have needed, your hand has provided." Not my hand, your hand. The scripture said in the 19th verse of the 6th chapter, "Storing up for themselves a good foundation for a time to come that they may lay hold on eternal life. What shall it profit a person if he gains the whole world and loses his own soul?" Or what shall a man give in exchange for his soul?"

You think about this little blink we call time. We are on this earth such an infinitesimal amount of time in relationship to forever. And what trash we trade our souls for. What filth, what emptiness that leaves us sad, in sorrow. The Bible talks about the pleasures of sin, it acknowledges that there is pleasure in sin, but it's for a short season. The season is short, if it lasts a hundred years, it's short. I had one of my kids talk to me the other day said something profound; he looked up at me and said, "Pastor, were you ever a little boy?" It seemed like yesterday. But I suspect it wasn't. Only one life, soon be passed. Only what's done for God will last.

Examine our hearts, be liberal to the kingdom of God, this world is falling apart. I read the Bible and I see the decline of America, because America really won't be a prominent part of prophecy. Some people try to make it that way, but it's just not in the Bible. The prominent players are going to be Russia and China, and it's going to be the anti-Christ through the European Union, but America is not there. We are declining, we are going downhill fast. And you know something, it's sad in a way because we have been a force for good in the world. But the Bible said, we're going to get so wrapped up - just like Israel did - in the pursuit of the lust of the flesh, lust of the eye and the pride of life, until God turns His back on us. Not as an individual, but as a nation. God never turns His back on His people, individually. Whatever we face, He faces it with us. But as a nation, we're going down, and all the pieces are in place for the church to be called into the presence of God.

Are you ready to meet God? Are you ready? And are you ready to live for God while you're here? Not just exist. You want the fullness of God in your life? Say no to materialism, say no to the lust of the flesh, say no to the pride of life, and say yes to Jesus. "Here I am, I am your bound servant, and I am here to do what you want me to do. I'll go where you want me to go, I'll say what you want me to say, I'll do what you want me to do Lord. I'm just your servant, and I'm so grateful that you love me enough to bring me into your kingdom and make me one of your own." And that's what contentment is.

SIXTEEN SERMONS

Sixteen prayers, from the Old and New Testament
A look at widely varied, flawed and imperfect prayers

Moses, Prayer of Complaint
Jabez, Prayer to Escape the Past
Jacob, Wrestling with God
King Asa, The Reformer Falls
Daniel, Prophetic Dreams and Interpretation
Disciples, Confronting their Fears
Disciples, Prayer in Persecution,
The Church, Prayer Flames the Church
The Widow: Weak Against the Strong
Disciples, Hanging On

By Pastor Louis Neely, taken from his forty-two years of pastoring Warehouse Christian Ministries, Sacramento, CA, a Calvary Chapel Affiliate Church

www.ingramcontent.com/pod-product-compliance
Lightning Source LLC
Chambersburg PA
CBHW021128300426
44113CB00006B/330